I Stand By The Door

Reflections About the Work of Evangelism

DR. ROBERT KLINE

Copyright 2020 by David Dean
All rights reserved
No part of this book may be reproduced or transmitted in any form or by any means, electronic or mechanical, including photocopying, recording, or by any information storage and retrieval system, without permission in writing from the copyright owner.

Scripture quotations marked KJV are taken from the Holy Bible, authorized King James Version unless otherwise noted.

To order additional copies of this book, contact:

Address all inquiries to
David Dean
21271 Wintergreen Drive
Circleville, Ohio 43113
www.amazon.com

For Worthwhile Books
FWB Publications

ISBN 9798623825575 Soft cover | Evangelism

I Stand By the Door

By Dr. Sam Shoemaker

I stand by the door.
I neither go too far in, nor stay too far out,
The door is the most important door in the world—
It is the door through which people walk when they find God.
There's no use my going way inside, and staying there,
When so many are still outside, and they, as much as I,
Crave to know where the door is.
And all that so many ever find
Is only the wall where a door ought to be.
They creep along the wall like those who are blind.
With outstretched, groping hands,
Feeling for a door, knowing there must be a door,
Yet they never find it . . .
So I stand by the door.

The most tremendous thing in the world
Is for people to find that door—the door to God.
The most important thing any one can do
Is to take hold of one of those blind, groping hands,
And put it on the latch—the latch that only clicks
And opens to one's own touch.
People die outside that door, as starving beggars die
On cold nights in cruel cities in the dead of winter—
Die for want of what is within their grasp.
They live, on the other side of it—live because they have found it.

Nothing else matters compared to helping them find it,
And open it, and walk in, and find Him . . .
So I stand by the door.

Go in, great saints, go all the way in—
Go way down into the cavernous cellars,
And way up into the spacious attics—
In a vast, roomy house, this house where God is.
Go into the deepest of hidden casements,
Of withdrawal, of silence, of sainthood.
Some must inhabit those inner rooms,
And know the depths and heights of God,
And call outside to the rest of us how wonderful it is.
Sometimes I take a deeper look in,
Sometimes venture a little farther;
But my place seems closer to the opening . . .
So I stand by the door.

The people too far in do not see how near these are
To leaving—preoccupied with the wonder of it all.
Somebody must watch for those who have entered the door,
But would like to run away. So for them, too,
I stand by the door.

I admire the people who go way in.
But I wish they would not forget how it was
Before they got in. Then they would be able to help
The people who have not even found the door,
Or the people who want to run away again from God.
You can go in too deeply, and stay in too long,
And forget the people outside the door.
As for me, I shall take my old accustomed place,
Near enough to God to hear Him, and know He is there,
But not so far from people as not to hear them,

And remember they are there too.
Where? Outside the door—
Thousands of them, millions of them.
But—more important for me—
One of them, two of them, ten of them,
Whose hands I am intended to put on the latch,
So I shall stand by the door and wait
For those who seek it.
'I had rather be a door-keeper . . .'
So I stand by the door.

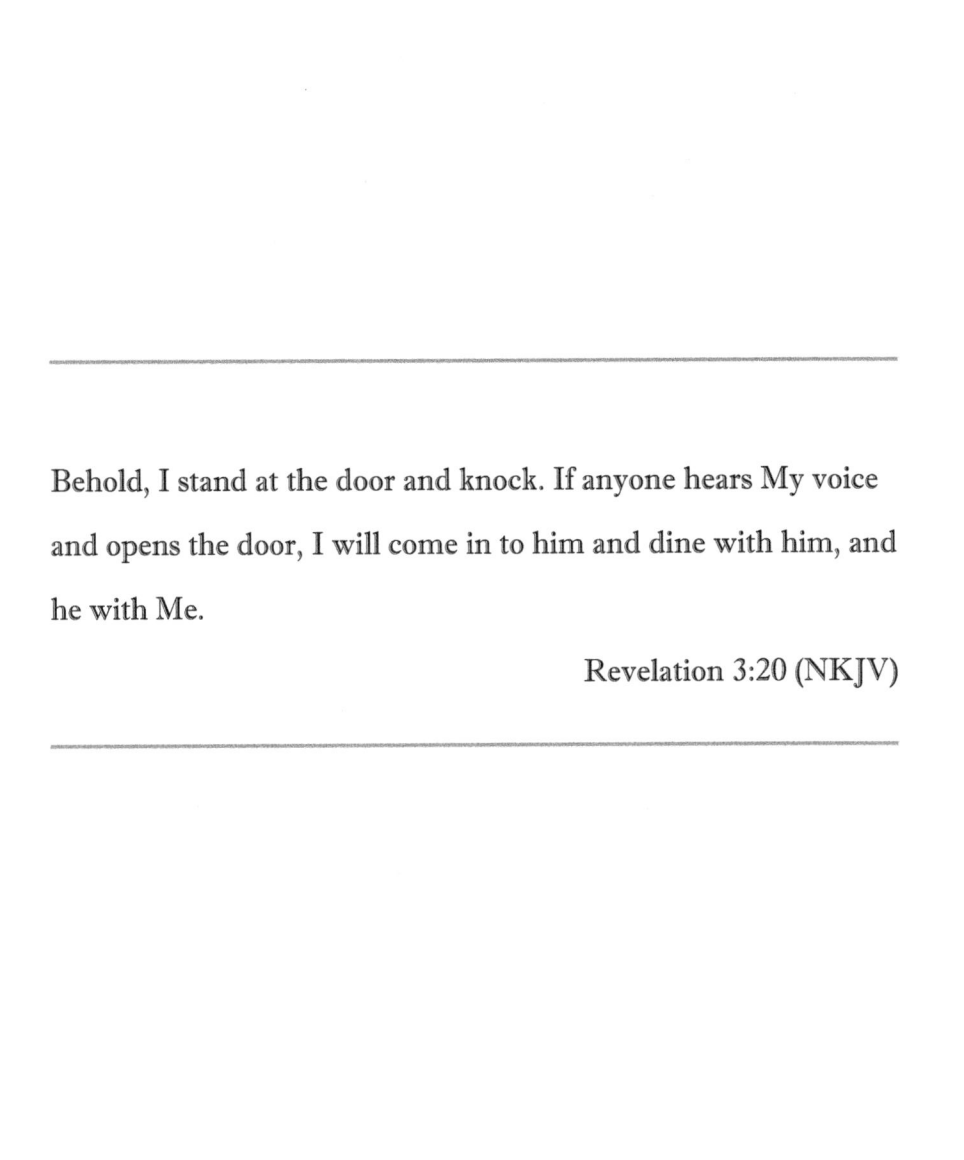

Behold, I stand at the door and knock. If anyone hears My voice and opens the door, I will come in to him and dine with him, and he with Me.

Revelation 3:20 (NKJV)

DEDICATION

It is with great joy and gratitude that we dedicate this book to one of the most remarkable women we have ever known,

Lediabelle Kline

She has demonstrated faith, love and perseverance through many years of suffering with Multiple Sclerosis. Her unwavering support of Dad enabled him to accomplish all he did in ministry over the years. He always said, "She was the strongest person he had ever known." And we, as her family, have found it to be true.

TRIBUTE

Dr. Robert Kline was one of the most influential leaders of his day. He served as the General Superintendent for the Churches of Christ in Christian Union from 1979-1990.

However, to us who knew him as Dad, Bob, Uncle Bob, or Grandpa, we saw a dimension of his life that many were not privileged to see. We always knew that his greatest love and commitment was to us, as his family.

Many other leaders became so involved in doing kingdom work that their families felt neglected. We never felt that way because he did not live that way. His greatest influence was upon those of us who knew him best. His Godly life, his wise counsel, and his unfailing love to all of us will never be forgotten.

His passion was to lead people to Christ and to then, help them grow in their faith.

It is with greatest joy that we, as the family, of Dr. Robert Kline present this book to you. The contents are just a few of the writings that were found in their house, some handwritten, some typed, and some saved on floppy disks. This project was truly a family project done with love and deepest respect for the one who helped lead all of us to become fully devoted followers of the Lord Jesus Christ.

May the Lord bless you in your journey.

Sincerely,

The Kline Family

TABLE OF CONTENTS

The Birth Of Evangelism 1

The Breath Of Evangelism 15

The Brokenness In Evangelism 31

The Bridge: Part One 49

The Bridge: Part Two 53

The Tyranny Of Tolerance 59

Beyond Forgiveness? 67

Birthing Baby Christians 73

Elijah: Worship And Mantles 81

Where Is The Lord God Of Elijah? 87

We Get What We Really Want. 95

The Common Prayer For The Uncommon 103

Hopelessness 109

THE BIRTH OF EVANGELISM

A nagging question eats at the heart and mind of many holiness people today. Armed with all the weaponry and tradition of an inherited theology we ask, "Why can't we, of all people, lead the way in evangelism? Finding no satisfactory answer, we busy ourselves with a "passion for definition" of a myriad of other issues. We desperately try to find fulfillment, but in our theology, it cannot be found without evangelism. It is an integral part of the whole. The result of whatever it is we are doing; it isn't attractive or challenging to the few converts to Christ we manage to win. While too many of us sit on the sideline seeking answers to questions no one is asking, millions of unreached people slip into a Christless eternity.

Germane to the issue is our concept of the lost. Do we sincerely have an unshakable conviction that unsaved people are really lost? The fuzzy mindset about the fate of a sinner so prevalent in the heart of holiness people today, is not unlike that of others in more liberal theological circles. Though not vocalized, it bleeds through church activities and philosophies that sometime, somewhere, somehow, God is going to usher everyone into the fold. There is no urgency. One could gather that few, deep down, believe in a literal hell. But lost people are lost! If not reached they will spend eternity separated from God. In order to reach lost people, we must believe they are hopeless without God. A Birth of Evangelism must occur in the human heart in order to successfully evangelize. It is not just a good idea. It is central to the doctrine of entire sanctification.

I Stand By The Door

I am convinced there is a missing dynamic in contemporary holiness theology. Without it, we give a scant evidence of a heart made pure. Holiness theology void of a heart for evangelism is a misnomer. We believe that true holiness should bring a pure heart. We also believe in the concept of power for service and for resisting temptation. To stop there is to break the heart of God. The missing dynamic has to do with passion, and without it evangelism will occur but little. The passion for souls is produced when we genuinely, scripturally, experience perfect love. Too long we have in all practicality tried to separate perfect love for God and perfect love for mankind.

They cannot be scripturally and experientially separated. Perfect love for God produces perfect love for people - the saved and unsaved. Perfect love for people produces a heart - a passion to evangelize. We fall in love with what Christ loves - the eternal souls of mankind. It is futile to repeatedly walk into the presence of God under the guise of some weird concept of worship and walk away with no sense of responsibility to rescue dying humanity from eternal punishment. It's a contradiction! It must be the ultimate in self-centeredness and arrogance. Such a response is foreign to a heart made perfect in love. Perfect love brings a Birth of Evangelism in the heart of committed Christians. Call it a defining moment, a life-changing experience, or whatever, the heart experiences a brokenness over unsaved people. Nothing less than this will take us to where we inwardly sense we ought to be.

Void of this, holiness people are rudderless, and stripped of any possibility of providing leadership to the general church today.

In a broad, general sense of the term, evangelism is born in the heart of God. He is the source. The heartbeat of God is evangelism. Otherwise, Calvary would never have happened. Christ, God's Son, was the sacrificial Lamb for the sins of humans. He was the Lamb slain from the foundation of the earth. *(Revelation 13:8) Behold, the Lamb of God, which taketh away the sins of the world. (John 1:29) For God so loved the world (the human race) that He gave His only begotten Son that whosoever believeth in Him should not perish but have everlasting life. (John 3:16)*

Without God's plan there would be no redemption for fallen, sinful man. Evangelism was born in the heart of God and He desires to reproduce in us. The seed of evangelism in the heart of God is sown in our hearts and He longs for germination and reproduction. It is housed in the plant of perfect love. Whatever is less than this has to do with either misplaced priorities or an erroneous interpretation of the sanctified life. Maybe some of both.

Every Christian can and should experience a Birth of Evangelism. It is the natural overflow and outflow of a wholesome, holy, heart. Jesus told His followers to not leave Jerusalem *until they received the promise of the Father. (Luke 24:49)* In Acts 1:8 He said just prior to His ascension, *you shall receive power after that the Holy Ghost is come upon you, <u>and you shall be witnesses unto Me</u> in Jerusalem, and in all Judea, and in Samaria, and unto the uttermost part of the earth.*

I hope sooner than later we will learn world evangelism is the normal flow of love out of a heart filled with perfect love for God and man, beginning next door. The Birth of Evangelism comes when the heart is in total surrender to God.

The call is not to commitment, but to surrender and that flies in the face of pop-theology. To attempt evangelism without this ultimately leads to frustration, burnout, and exhaustion. *That which is of the flesh is flesh and that which is of the Spirit is Spirit.* Evangelism in the flesh in unnatural. Evangelism in the Spirit is the norm.

Jesus was asked, *Which is the greatest commandment? (Matthew 22:36)* His response, *Thou shalt love the Lord thy God with all thy heart, and with all thy soul, and with all thy mind. This is the first and great commandment. And the second is like unto it, Thou shalt love thy neighbor as thyself. On these two commandments hang all the law and the prophets. (Matthew 22:37, 40) Thou shalt love the Lord thy God, with all thy heart, and with all thy soul, and with all thy mind, and with all thy strength: This is the first commandment. And the second is like, namely this, thou shalt love thy neighbor as thyself. There is none other commandment greater than these. (Mark 12: 30, 31) And behold a certain lawyer stood up, and tempted Him saying, Master, what shall I do to inherit eternal life? He said unto him, What is written in the law? How readest thou? And he answering said, Thou shalt love the Lord thy God with all thy heart, and with all thy soul, and with all thy strength, and with all thy mind, and thy neighbor as thyself. And He said unto him, Thou hast answered right, this do, and thou shalt live. (Luke 10:25, 28)*

In Jesus' response, each of the three Gospels written verifies His tying the two commandments together. Not unlike many today the "certain lawyer" asked, *Who is my neighbor? (Luke 10:29)* Jesus illustrated His answer by giving the parable of the Good Samaritan. The priest and Levite seeing and ignoring the wounded traveler are symbolic of unconcerned Christians today. We see the lost, we know their plight. We could help, but we are busy doing other things. Church things. The Samaritans saw him, came to him, had compassion for him. He lifted him, took him to a lodging place, and paid for his care. He typifies the heart made perfect in love.

While we revel in our experiences with God, and are content to do only that, Satan ravages the lives of people down the street. False cults are now reaching multiplied thousands with a message that offers little if any hope of salvation from sin. In desperation for something to believe in, the masses are embracing whatever is offered. The one desire of the hungry is for food. The table is set across the world - but the hungry hunger on. We have people in every direction that can be won to Christ now! The fields are ripe, and they have not ripened by accident. God has cultivated and ripened them. He's calling for harvesters. He wants the fields reaped. I know I could face criticism for saying it, but Christians must question and resist anti-harvest people wherever we find them. The Great Commission to go and preach the Gospel to everyone is still in effect. It isn't just a challenge or for a select few, it is a charge given by our Lord. We love to major on His promises, but minor on His charge to evangelize lost people.

It is God's will that we reach the lost, but we are not taking Him seriously. From childhood, we have heard about a Christian's responsibility to win others to Christ. We have been told how the blood of the untold of our generation will be on our hands in the day of judgment. We know! That is not the problem. Weak links are caused in the chain of evangelism because of the wide gap between what we often profess and what we possess.

Is the lack of power, a dearth of spiritual fervor, and the shunning of evangelistic responsibility because we, in all honesty, have nothing to give away? I really hope not. But, such a small percentage of Christians have ever led a soul home to Christ. This should not happen to holiness people. Our love for God should translate into a fervent love for souls.

We must go to the lost! Sunday after Sunday, well-meaning people cry out for them to come. This is right, but it should be preceded by a heeding of Christ's command to "go out into the highways and hedges." Go into every section of the community with the message that "Jesus loves and saves." When the church building complex serves as the base of operation, and our communities are the fields of work, they synchronize. But, when the church facility becomes both the base and the field, the harvest is questionable if not impossible. I have a fear that many of our programs and resources today have inadvertently become at best a hindrance, and at worst, the enemy of evangelism. We have had an over-emphasis on what happens in the church facility at the expense of soul winning. The lost do not hear and if they could, they could care less about much of what is prioritized.

The Wesleyan revival produced personal witnessing. John Wesley told his preachers, "You have nothing to do but win souls." He would be called narrow today. Do not question his results! Regardless of the weather or circumstances, the Methodists paths led them to the homes of the unsaved. They believed, and we must believe, that one cannot be truly sanctified wholly without a passion for souls. Their trail was well marked with changed hearts, homes, and communities. They ministered to the whole person.

Their perfect love for God resulted in a mighty demonstration of perfect love for mankind. Kingdom growth was the product. Churches were planted across the landscape. A Birth of Evangelism was a reality in their hearts.

The Cycle of Revival and Evangelism

Church history proves there are periods of evangelism crises. Churches rise and fall. Denominations and para-church organizations rise and fall. Life - spiritual life, is involved. They grow old and die! Only a miracle can bring reproduction to a woman past the age of fertility. The same principle applies to the Church. Where are the strong, flourishing New Testament churches today? Only churches that evangelize and reproduce survive. A cycle of revival and evangelism is involved. Churches, like individuals, must cultivate growth - life. New births come in times of revival and concern. Apathy, carelessness, and neglect prohibit evangelism and growth.

Every true New Testament church was born in the fires of revival. Evangelism was a high priority. In the process of growth, the church climbs to a peak. Discipling converts becomes a vital part of the program. Excitement prevails as baby Christians are born into the church family. Sacrifice is a given during this dramatic era. However, in every local church's history, the seeds of institutionalism are soon sown. Church growth amazingly attracts non-growth people. They are often affluent and influential families. They are elected to boards and committees. They eventually introduce and will fight for programs that are of little value to a church whose Mission Statement surges with evangelism. Tension begins between growth and non-growth people.

Compromise is inevitable unless a genuine revival occurs at this juncture. An evangelism crisis clouds the horizon of that church.

An exciting revival spirit and evangelism fervor is the first to exit. It is often a subtle shift, but the congregation drifts into a non-growth mode. Sufficient funds are available to build buildings and pay the pastor. The church becomes an influence in the community. The congregation is respectable. The paradigm has shifted. Transfer growth replaces reproduction growth. The programs are sharpened until the public services are superb. The denomination will applaud the stability of the church. The pastor and church become the model for other small churches. Budgets are paid in full. Denominational oversight is unneeded.

However, the seed of institutionalism are growing, and they are the seeds of decay and death. At this point, the options are either legalism or liberalism. In the process doctrinal lines become hazy because either one produces a debilitating blow to the effectiveness and life of a church. The church was born in the fires of evangelism and revival. The fire is out. The people are busy doing church stuff. New and more elaborate programs are begun, but they are only connected to the original Mission Statement by a wide stretch of one's imagination. It is a shift from the pioneer revival and evangelism syndrome that produced true growth, to a maintenance program, that pulls a congregation into decay and death. When a local church survives and grows by membership transfer it is in the decay and coldness part of the cycle of revival and evangelism. That church may be the pride of the church community and the denomination, but in truth, it is in the process of self-destruction.

I Stand By The Door

One inner doctrinal or relationship problem will evidence its state quickly. One larger church with the same philosophy that is nearby will eventually empty it.

What really happened? As I see it every church, soon after its birth, is divided into three core groups of people. The first is the foundation on which the whole was built. They are solid, committed, evangelistic-minded people. Their presence is what attracted others. They design programs that fit their philosophy and the church grows. They are visionary and aggressive in nature. The second group is the non-growth minded. They were drawn to the church because of the excitement, but their philosophy is in direct opposition to the growth oriented. They are powerful personalities, and in time move into leadership. They too are committed and will gain strength in the inevitable power struggle. In order not to lose people, a compromise is made. The two groups honestly attempt to peacefully co-exist. They cannot indefinitely. Historically, the non-growth parts of the core wrest the leadership from the opposition. The battle for all practical purposes is over. The church resigns itself to the status quo and mediocrity. At this point, it measures itself not by the New Testament model, but by other similar contemporary churches.

The third group consists of followers. They are, at heart, mostly non-evangelistic people, but they float to the dominant style of leadership in the church. They will at times, if popular, become spiritually involved. They are other times disconnected and unfaithful. Little really challenges them. The tragedy is they ultimately cast the deciding vote as to what direction the congregation will move. They are satisfied with the size of the church at whatever level. They are unstable doctrinally.

I Stand By The Door

They may at times, volunteer for service, but only after a personal crisis. They are important because there is strength in numbers, and they are part of the mix. This group is usually in a state of flux and may move to another church upon the least provocation. They want to be serviced and will transfer out when another church provides this.

Can a church, once they have shifted to a maintenance mode, return to the growth part of the cycle? It has been done, but it is unlikely. The price is considered too great. The evangelistic group has either succumbed or moved to another church. Biological growth is at a minimum. The personnel resources required are scarce. No longer is the leadership aware of the possibilities, nor do they have the desire to change. However, it can and occasionally does occur.

One of the by-products of a church or denomination leaving revival and evangelism is a spin-off. The growth people will migrate out of the circle. It often results in the planting of another church. Across the years of church history, it has produced the forming of a new denomination. Denominationalism has taken its criticism. It is always in vogue. However, when the mother church leaves her distinctives and drifts to a liberal stance doctrinally, it is my belief that God can be the force behind the spin-off. It may not always be true, but it happens.

I also believe that once a denomination shifts from an evangelistic philosophy, God will bring to birth one that is in the fire and evangelism part of the cycle. It almost must happen. God will build His church, and, in His wisdom. He obviously must prompt some dramatic events. He will birth some new pioneers.

I Stand By The Door

Another one of the by-products of a church leaving revival and evangelism is a leadership crisis. A growth-minded pastor seldom can conform to a non-growth church. Nor can a maintenance-oriented pastor feel comfortable in a growing, evangelistic congregation. The two philosophies are poles apart. The result in either situation is a crisis.

In the history of most churches, there is a place for both the builder-pioneer and the maintenance pastor. The broader cycle of the church will have periods when stability and healing must occur. The church, though growth-oriented, has gone through a season of storms. This suffering body of believers must have time and help to recover. They cannot be aggressive in evangelism in such a state. Baby Christians cannot be birthed. Expansion is not now the issue.

A pastor, gifted in healing and encouragement, is needed. He can be a healer-leader. Members will find it easy to bond with him and the process of recovery will begin. He is at home and comfortable in this setting. His gifts and passions are designed for this. God will use him to stabilize the congregation. Losses will be minimized. The membership will move from negative to positive attitudes. Because of the bitter storm, and a God-sent pastor, endowed with much needed leadership skills, the church will become stronger and return to evangelism. May our Lord give us more of such valuable pastor-leaders.

A builder-pioneer pastor will suffer and be ill at ease in a maintenance-oriented church. He is aggressive, and maybe at times offensive in his approach. The fire to win lost people is hot. Evangelism is his meat and he has little sympathy for those who are apathetic and lazy about outreach. His messages are centered in soul winning.

He will inevitably attempt to change the course, sometimes with or without followers. He feels he will incur God's wrath if he fails. Board meetings are a nightmare. He will push until the church often divides, and pressure is on him and his family. When a church is in the cold, passive, maintenance mode, and a builder-pioneer style pastor assumes the leadership role, a disaster is in the making. We must understand where the local church is in the cycle of evangelism and select proper leadership for that time. Pastors and congregations have suffered injuries and carry scars into next generations due to an unsuitable mix.

Again, can a church, once they move from an evangelistic mode, change? Can they ever return to a thriving, exciting, soul-winning body of believers? I have to say it is unlikely, but possible. When the pastor and a segment of the membership begin to hunger for a return, it can happen. What produced the original fire can re-occur. If God can do it once, He can do it again. It will not be easy because the church has a history of satisfaction with a maintenance style. Not all the people will want or see the need to make a change. But it can happen. In this shift, tension will surface between growth and non-growth forces. I know God can and will come. Yet, the decision will be made according to degree of desire to change.

It all begins with a spiritual awakening. People begin to realize what has happened to the church and are concerned. Tension between growth and non-growth forces will evidence. But prayer is now a high priority. The suffering that naturally accompanies birth must be endured. God begins to bring the fires of revival. The cold, calculating attitudes, begin warming. Restitutions are made.

I Stand By The Door

Relationships that were damaged in such an environment begin to heal. Priorities are re-arranged. An honest look is made regarding existing programs. A rediscovery of the lostness of the lost brings a sense of guilt for the apathy in human hearts. Forgiveness from God is sought as we realize how far away, we are from loving Him. Revival fires heat up. God pulls us away from the debris and we get a clear look as to where He wants to take us. Only perfect love for Him can produce the love we need to reach out to lost people. It is a new beginning! Exciting, but humbling. Fulfilling. When the Holy Spirit comes in His fullness, we experience the Birth of Evangelism. Ears to hear the voice of God. Eyes to see the lost. A passion to reach them.

When the Holy Spirit came upon the Virgin Mary, she conceived and brought forth a Son. When the Church travails, she also brings forth children. This is a type of the Holy Spirit coming upon us. Spiritual reproduction becomes the norm for a healthy, fertile, Christian. The seed of love is in the heart of God that gives birth to the plant of evangelism. Calvary is the ultimate result. He wants to reproduce in us. He houses it in the seed of perfect love. It can germinate and grow or lay dormant in the soil of the human heart. It is up to us and requires a death if the plant flourishes. Death to self-centeredness, pride and whatever else is foreign to a heart made perfect in love, must occur. "If it dies, it will bring forth fruit." Something of beauty will be born, a perfect love for mankind that results in a holy passion to reach the lost. We will love them too much to let them slip into eternity without telling them about Christ's love. We have experienced a Birth of Evangelism, and it can change a church.

I Stand By The Door

THE BREATH OF EVANGELISM

It is life or death! As specie can become extinct without reproduction, so a church can die unless they reproduce. Churches and denominations are in the state of decay due to a lack of fire and evangelism. When the Holy Spirit breathed into the early church, she bore children. Only when the Holy Spirit comes on the church <u>can</u> she reproduce. The test of our condition is, are we producing healthy new Christians to the extent that true growth occurs? They are always born in the warm, wholesome womb of a God-filled heart. Church growth is no mystery, it is the natural result of spiritual conception and reproduction.

A mother must endure the pain of childbirth in order to bring a beautiful baby into the world. If spiritual children are to be born, someone must step up and accept the travail for the salvation of eternal souls. In earnest prayer, a passion for evangelism will bring forth a new life into the Kingdom. There is no other way. God ordained no other plan. If so, why are there so few Christians that are committed to soul winning? The <u>silent</u> <u>debate</u> in holiness churches today is over evangelism. It will probably never reach a convention or seminar floor, but it is the debate.

Whoever wins will determine the destiny of the modern day, holiness movement. It will play out in local churches, not in denominational headquarters.

The reasons are many for the utter lack of personal evangelism. The culture, the mood of the generation and a kind of "spiritual correctness" are all involved.

It is not now "correct" in the church to aggressively pursue reaching lost people for Christ. It is considered fun to tell stories about personal soul winners. It will always break up the crowd. We are encouraged to "indirectly" crowd people to Christ. It is known in the field and science of selling as "soft sell." The church is always decades behind the world. The secular sales organization abandoned this when it was found to be non-productive. Too many great corporations were brought to their knees and sales forces were "jerked to reality" by the stockholders. The new philosophy was the resurrection of the old and people hit the streets and talked to people. Some never survived. Merger rescued some others.

Lifestyle evangelism, and I believe in it with all my heart, has taken the field at the exclusion of intentional, deliberate, programs to reach lost people. It has never been one or the other - it takes both. Our record of winning lost people to Christ indicates more must be done. Every Christian must feel the Breath of Evangelism. It is the channel through which God extends His great love toward fallen humanity. Obedient hearts, however humble and limited, are the conduits. The flow of His love swept on by the Breath of Evangelism moves men to God and God to man. It leaps oceans, crosses denominational lines, and penetrates crusted cultures. It can only be stopped when Christians stop it. *Jesus spoke about it prior to His ascension, Ye shall receive power, after that the Holy Ghost is come upon you, and ye shall be witnesses unto Me both in Jerusalem, and in all Judea, and in Samaria, and unto the uttermost part of the earth. (Acts 1:8)*

The Breath of Evangelism provides both the power and the program for the church to evangelize.

The power is the Holy Spirit. The Greek word for power in Acts 1:8 is "dynamis", translated "dynamite-dynamo." He, the Holy Spirit, is the power-means-might-strength, and force that enables us to be witnesses. Even in what is called a "post-Christian era." This happened to the first century church at Pentecost. The disciples knew more about evangelism thirty minutes after Pentecost than all their life before. Evangelism is what they did. It was not just a priority. This is who they were. Three thousand souls were saved in one day, in the very face of religious and political opposition. When we "become who we really are", power comes from another world. "You shall be witnesses", Jesus said.

The program of the church is too obvious to miss. They left the Upper Room in Jerusalem with only one plan – the evangelization of the world. It is important to understand they started where they were, in Jerusalem. The reason for their success in recruiting workers for the harvest is they did not *"go to the fields"* - they were *"in them."* Mission organizations will never have enough missionaries to staff foreign fields unless harvesters are reaping as they go. It is also true here at home. Churches will suffer because of a lack of God-called pastors and workers when we do not win souls. The pastors and missionaries for the next generation are yet to become Christians. It is possible to be active in the church and yet not be productive. We can borrow workers. We can trade workers. We can buy workers. We can hire workers, but the ripened fields will not be harvested unless more workers are produced.

That happens in local churches, and it is going to be decided by the winner of the "silent debate."

I Stand By The Door

We have never known so much about "church" before. We know the principles of church growth. We study the studies about successful churches. We listen to speakers hours upon hours about everything from computers to suitable parking lots. An addition of fifty or less new parishioners send us frantically into derision. We know how to design agendas and form committees. We have information libraries and the Internet until our heads are overloaded. We are "choking" on plans, programs and ideas. We have had enough information shoved into our minds to reach the whole world tomorrow, if that would do it. We are organized to do whatever it is we are doing. I am impressed! Yet, I fear all the above could become the message and not the method. Lost in the stack of helps and procedures is a simple plan and power to reach into Satan's world and rescue dying humanity from eternal punishment. Holiness people, doctrinally, embody the answer if we believe what we ought to be preaching – perfect love for God and mankind. This carried on the winds of the Breath of Evangelism can enable us to be His "witnesses."

In Acts 1:8, the word power (dynamis) works in two areas. We first have the power not to sin, we do not have to disobey Him. We can will not to disobey a known law of God. We can resist temptation and be over-comers. He provides the "power" to persevere and triumph. We, with the help of the Holy Spirit, can elect not to succumb to Satan. Moment by moment, we can have victory over his designs. Our heart can be left with a pure desire to please Christ. Our heart can say, *"not my will – but Christ's be done."* Because of this supernatural power, we can be victorious!

Caving into Satan's plans is not on our agenda because we have surrendered to Christ.

Acts 1:8 also mentions the power to witness. We, after surrendering of our heart and mind to Christ, have the enduement of power to wins souls. "*You shall be witnesses.*" He did not say some would, or at times, we might. He said, "Your very life will witness to the world that you are mine." It was a natural flow of love from Christ to Christians that is meant to flow on out to a lost world. *And I will put my Spirit within you. (Ezekiel 36:27) And I will put my Spirit within you, and you shall live. (Ezekiel 37:14) And, it shall come to pass afterward that I will pour my Spirit upon all flesh. (Joel 2:28)*

The word "Spirit" in the above scriptures could be translated "wind" or "breath." *God breathed into the nostrils of man the breath of life; and he became a living soul. (Genesis 2:7)* Breath is life. The Spirit brings life to what was once "dead plans and programs." We can beautify them, refine them, propagate them, but without the Spirit, they only further the process of decay and death in the church.

The word "wind" is the same word for "storm wind", signifying power. Wind can uproot trees and demolish buildings. It can also drive a ship. The Holy Spirit enters mankind and brings life. He brings power to what was weak. His breath breathes the wind in us that produces the power to cut across the grain of a hard, cold, heart, and plant the seed of love.

It is God's will that we earnestly seek the experience of true holiness that secures this power. *And behold, I send the promise of My Father upon you; but tarry ye in the city of Jerusalem, until ye be endued with power from on high. (Luke 24:49)* The program for the church is seen in this chapter.

The Evangelistic Message of the church is clearly stated. It is the age-old message of repentance and forgiveness through the atoning work of Christ. *And said unto them, thus it is written, and thus it behoved Christ to suffer, and to rise from the dead the third day. (Luke 24:46)* Even today in a nearby city, preacher-theologians are debating the validity of the resurrection of Jesus Christ. There is an offence to the Cross. If one would dare to follow Christ and suffer with Him for the sake of the gospel, he will be called narrow and legalistic. But, contrary to some "want to be" theologians, the way of the Cross leads home. It is time to understand that everyone is not sure of that and they have an audience. The resurrection is also a stumbling block to some. In an effort to be accepted, we could compromise here. Don't! He arose from the grave with the keys of death, hell and the grave chained to His girdle. His resurrection is a validation of His sacrifice and messiahship. This is the Evangelistic Message of the Church.

The Evangelistic Mandate is shared with us. *And that repentance and remission of sins should be preached in His name, among all nations, beginning at Jerusalem. (Luke 24:47)* The call from the heart of God to the church is "go." This is the mandate. It is irrevocable! We may ignore it. We may try to rationalize it away. We can crowd it out of our agendas, but not in the will of God.

The reason the unsaved do not come is because we do not go. It is more than a language we can learn or an option for Christians. These are not just some "old paths" out of a valueless tradition. They are the words of the One we will one day stand before and give an account of our stewardship. We know the Evangelistic Mandate.

Jesus is thorough. He gives us the Evangelistic Method. *And you are witnesses of these things. (Luke 24:48)* The world can only be reached as Christians give witness of their transformation. *And who is he that will harm you if ye be followers of that which is good? But if ye suffer for righteousness' sake, happy are ye; and be not afraid of their terror, neither be troubled. But sanctify the Lord in your hearts; and <u>be ready always to give an answer (witness) to every man that asketh you a reason of the hope that is in you</u> with meekness and fear. (I Peter 3:13, 15)* We are not given the task of saving the lost, we are to witness. The method is to tell – not just one another, but the lost. Some will hear and gladly respond in faith. Others will turn away. In our witness we must be obedient. The results are to be left with our Lord.

Jesus then spells out the Evangelistic Means. *And, behold, I send the promise of My Father upon you; but tarry (wait) ye in the city of Jerusalem until ye be endued with power from on high. (Luke 24:49)* In His conversation with Nicodemus, Jesus used an interesting Hebrew word, "ruach." It meant the Spirit of God, and also wind. It stood basically for three things. It meant "breath." This could have to do with life. It could also mean "desert wind or energy and force." In its meaning of the Spirit of God, Jesus used the word to illustrate the New Birth. It was the Breath of Evangelism to Nicodemus in John 3.

Jesus said to him, *The wind bloweth. (John 3:8)* This represents the ceaseless action of the Breath of Evangelism. In Genesis 1:2, it says, *The <u>Spirit</u> of God moved on the face of the waters.* In the Bible's last chapter, He says, *And the <u>Spirit</u> and the bride say come. And let him (everyone) that heareth say, come. And let him that is athirst come. And whosoever will, let him take the water of life freely. (Revelation 22:17)*

I Stand By The Door

The Psalmist cried, *Whither shall I go from thy <u>Spirit</u>? Or whither shall I flee from Thy presence? (Psalm 139:7)* At Pentecost, *And suddenly there came a sound from heaven as of a <u>rushing mighty wind</u>, and it filled all the house where they were sitting. (Acts 2:2)* The wind started blowing, moving men and women across the world. Jesus said, *"The wind blows."* In every generation the wind of the Spirit is felt. Before anyone confronts another about the claims of Christ, the Spirit is there. He precedes and accompanies His faithful witnesses. *"The wind blows."*

Jesus then said further, *The wind blows where it listeth* – where it will. Note the sovereign freedom of the Breath of Evangelism. Institutionalism has tried to close doors. It is impossible! It goes where it will. The Church has historically compartmentalized society when it comes to evangelism. It cannot be done. The unreachable are often the reached. The Breath of Evangelism crashes through man-made barriers and leaves our toys littered along the Gospel road. It overcomes obstacles. It blows where it will, and so often sweeps into unlikely places and people. According to man's standards some churches that are growing should not be. They defy the boxes the general church has tried to put them in. They break out. The Breath of Evangelism "confounds the wise and makes wise the simple." It will blow where it can. At times our well-oiled, and highly touted, little plans and programs shut it out. We can do that. At other times because of dry tradition, or a smug, self-satisfied congregation, it can stop the wind of the Spirit. He wants to fill and empower every Christian. He goes where He can and will.

Jesus told Nicodemus, *You hear the sound of the wind.* We can see the evidence of the Breath of Evangelism. The wind will always make its presence known.

I Stand By The Door

We see the "moving of leaves on the trees." We see its influence. An alcoholic becomes sober and cleans up his life. The prostitute becomes pure. Chronic liars clean up their act and become truthful. The addict is delivered and goes home again. Homes are rebuilt. Preachers and laymen become soul-winners.

Jesus then said, *And you cannot tell where the wind started.* The Breath of Evangelism is supernatural in its origin. It comes! And it changes! Explain Pentecost apart from the Breath of Evangelism. The 120 were hiding behind closed doors in Jerusalem *"for fear of the Jews."* After the wind of the Spirit swept through the Upper Room where they were gathered, they were accused of "turning the city upside down." When faced with potential death for their witness they said, *We will obey God rather than man.* Explain the dramatic conversions of Saul of Tarsus apart from the Breath of Evangelism. He was present at the stoning of Stephen and the wind began to blow. It climaxed when on the Damascus road he was stopped in his tracks. He became a leader of the newly born Christian church.

Explain the Wesleyan revival apart from the Breath of Evangelism. A clergyman in the Church of England was confronted with some real followers of Christ. In a service on Aldersgate Street, he heard an exposition on the book of Romans, and God lit a fire in his heart. His influence affects you and me yet today. Explain once lethargic preachers and laymen that are now totally involved in world missions apart from the Breath of Evangelism. Listen and you will hear the sound of the wind from heaven.

Jesus went on in His conversation with Nicodemus. *You cannot tell where the wind goes.* Do we today have a clue as to where the Breath of Evangelism will go?

I Stand By The Door

I don't think so. Who can tell the destiny of a soul winner when he feels the wind of the Spirit? The Upper Room crowd, once afraid and discouraged, were transformed. Thirty-some years later Christianity had swept through Asia Minor; Antioch became a great, growing church. It had penetrated to Egypt, and the Christians were making their mark in Alexandria. It leaped the sea, came to Rome, and moved through Greece. No one, including the disciples before Pentecost could have believed Christianity would spread like an unstoppable prairie fire throughout the world.

Pastors and missionaries, sometimes from humble beginnings, have been carried to the ends of the earth with Christ's message. There is no place safer than in the flow of the moving of the wind of the Spirit when He sends us. We need to be in the place to feel this gale from the heart of God. He is moving across the nation and around the world. Multiplied thousands are now responding to Jesus Christ in genuine faith.

Is there a price for the power Jesus spoke about in Luke 24:49 and Acts 1:8? If so, what is it? The price of power is "giving up." *Except a corn of wheat fall into the ground and die, it abideth alone, but if it dies, it will bring forth fruit. (John 12:24)* Deep in the heart of many holiness people today lies a hunger for such power. The needs all around are evident. Too many churches stumble through weeks of activities that have little to do, if anything, with the Mandate of the Church. Our adequacies can become our most conspicuous inadequacy. Man, apart from the power of the Spirit, is rendered helpless in winning lost people to Christ. But the power comes at a high price – maybe too high for the church at the end of this century.

I Stand By The Door

The Upper Room crowd finally came to understand that by "giving up" they became the recipients of the means to evangelize.

What did they leave in that Upper Room? Everything! How paradoxical! They were emptied of everything and left with it all. They cut a new trail of evangelism across the known world. They were in the flow of the Breath of Evangelism. It cost many of them their life and possessions. If we are to be soul winners today, we will walk in their tracks wherever the Spirit leads.

I know of nothing more exciting than a church that is on fire to win souls. Most problems in any church could be solved by winning some new converts to Christ. It is strange that somewhere in our history we stopped keeping records of the number of new converts. We elect people to offices in local churches for everything from Sunday School to the flower fund. And we should. But evangelism, the task of the church, is without a sponsor or representative on the local church board. I do not believe this is intentional. I do believe we are wrong to assume it will be done, and that it will always be a vital part of the church programs. It only takes one generation to crowd it off the agenda. It becomes lost in the sea of activities. In order to ensure evangelism in the local church, it must move to the highest in our priorities. When this is done, not everyone, but someone will have the high level of responsibility to promote evangelism. They should, by virtue of their office, be a member of the local church board. A Department of Evangelism is long overdue in our system.

Most churches adopted a Mission Statement some years ago. It was the thing to do to be "correct." However, most Mission Statements and programs in local churches are not even remotely connected.

I Stand By The Door

The Mission Statement was an announcement that the church was "with the program." To not do it was unacceptable. What we do or not do tells who we really are, not Mission Statements. The "silent debate" has had more to do with our real activities than anything else. It has moved us from evangelism to an introverted style of church. Our emphasis has been on us and ours. We have "over-loaded" on worship style. The Sunday Morning service has become a production for entertainment. Whoever has the most toys win, and transfer growth continues, and the crowd applauds. Something is wrong in Zion.

Ladies and Gentlemen, with billions of unreached people, we must not be content with the status-quo. The Church has her grandest opportunity to shine a beacon of hope into a darkened world. People of all ages, in and out of the church are troubled about current events. They are searching for answers. What the secular humanists offered does not meet the deep, inner need of humanity. It is still "sick from the top of his head, to the sole of his feet", crying for a touch that will heal his disease.

War clouds hover over strategic, prophecy-centered areas of the world despite the genius of military and negotiation strategists. Our own nation is now feeling the results of terrorism. Travelers fear now as their journeys take them around the globe. Crime and violence are now part of our lifestyle from the inner city to rural areas.

When I hear it all I am reminded of Christ's words, *Heaven and earth may pass away, but my words shall not pass away.* Thank God, some things remain, when worlds and heavens are tossed like a leaf in a storm. The Church, with her message of salvation, peace and hope, has never been needed more.

I Stand By The Door

Troubled minds and hearts have always been fertile soil for evangelism.

The "silent debate" is a debate, not one-sided. I am encouraged by the growing burden and vision I see in the heart of some today. They want growth. They know souls must be won. We must give vent to this spirit that is beginning to build. I am hearing a cry for revival among our people and they are involved in intercessory prayer. This is right, but it is not enough. We must "move on to the next level" and feel the wind of the Spirit as He presses us to leave our knees and go out into the streets and persuade people to come to Christ. Now is the time for an offensive move. Someone has said, "A good defense is the best offense." We have been on the defensive long enough. We have no defense if we fail to launch a mighty offensive move at this time. Pornography and obscenity now pour over our nation like an ugly river out of control. Child prostitution is now a multi-billion dollar a year business. The television industry is invading homes and shattering principles and ethics that we know are not right. The courts of our land are largely staffed with immoral people and presently make the nation's decisions as to what is right and wrong.

When one out of four children will be sexually molested before they enter high school, something is wrong. When incest, sexual perversions, and child abuse is epidemic it is time to make a change. The true church must be broken-hearted – angry, at what is happening.

Senseless murders occur now in daylight. Rape is common. More than 100 million people will fall asleep hungry tonight. If they do survive the hunger and inclement weather, they face the same tomorrow.

I Stand By The Door

It is no wonder the "under-dog in the silent debate" is feeling the burden and concern. The world is lost! Do not lose your sense of "the lost-ness of lost people." Or "holy compassion" for lost humanity. A revival we have been praying for could be on its way. And from it world evangelization! It will not originate in the flesh. It will come down out of heaven like a mighty torrent, yet soft as a summer breeze. I pray it will fill every valley and cover every hill. It will uproot sin in the heart of men and women.

Today we stand on the little edge of what could be the greatest advance the church has ever made. May we be willing to pay the price to see an all-out offensive battle against the forces of evil. I somehow feel God's army will be on the march with or without us. God will not be defeated! The winds of change and crisis are blowing the church from its safe and sheltered position and only God knows where the Breath of Evangelism will take us.

Jesus demonstrated His faith in humanity long ago. How could He expect a few, faulty men, unlearned and self-seeking to be the means of remaking the world? They failed Him in His darkest hours. They slept in the Garden. They fled like frightened sheep when He was arrested. He was doubted. All were blind to the beauty of His character. Yet, knowing their cowardice and shortcomings, Jesus put the responsibility of world conquest on their shoulders. He proclaimed to the world, *The gates of hell shall not prevail against it. [Matthew 16:18]* And soon they spread His message of salvation across the world. He, as amazing as it sounds, believes in us today. Incredible! And, what we do, in His name, under His leadership, and in His power will outlive us.

I Stand By The Door

This gives enduring grace when our little world falls apart and our best decided plans lay at our feet in ashes. What we are doing is "lifting an eternal beacon of light and hope out over an angry sea for shipwrecked humanity." It is "offering bread to the mass of spiritually hungry beggars that walk the winding roads of earth." Praise God! What we are doing will change the world – and live on – and stretch into eternity for God and good.

There may be some seasons of temporary plateaus and minimal gains. But our God is sovereign. He answers to no man and yet He answers to every man, woman, boy and girl that comes before Him in faith. We cannot fail when we have done our best, because He cannot fail. We are linked to Him in purpose. We can face the power of Satan because our objectives are bound up in God. He has overcome! So, we will overcome! In our efforts to stand and reach the unreached.

The wind from the Breath of Evangelism is still blowing. It may be a gentle breeze – but the wind is blowing. Let's catch it and ride it out. Who knows what will happen?

I Stand By The Door

THE BROKENNESS IN EVANGELISM

It is either a garden or a game. To some of the crowd, Christianity is a Sunday morning thing. A social event, an obligation, or a game people play. They sing the songs, give token offerings, and help raise the applause level for whomever is cheerleading in the public services. When the pastor delivers a sermon that aims at no one, and appeals to most, they lead the line to extend a compliment. They are religious, but really, church and God are just a diversion in their life. A rough, strenuous week on the job will bring them to church on Sunday mornings. It is the thing to do as long as it doesn't interfere with other activities. But, for the way it might appear to others, church wouldn't necessarily be a part of their schedule. It's a game some people play that serves as an oasis from the monotony of home and career.

Christianity is a garden to another part of the crowd. Though it may have beautiful surroundings, the garden is a place of suffering. No game! Nor a performance! These people walk away from the crowd and enter a place not many are willing to go. For Jesus, it was the Garden of Gethsemane. Decisions are made here that will set life's course. There is an aloneness in the garden. Here we are stripped of the veneer and kneel before a Sovereign God in total submission. Or, we can walk away. Most do.

Here the forces of good and evil clash. God and Satan meet head on. We're the subject of the battle, and we decide the outcome. Too many try to advance to a cross without going to the garden. They are ill prepared. No garden, no cross. No cross, no victory.

I Stand By The Door

A brokenness in the heart must come if we are to enter life's best. Only when a brokenness in our evangelism occurs can we have what we need to rescue dying humanity from eternal punishment. Anything less is just a game. Battles are not won in the game, but in the garden.

Jesus and His disciples had finished the Last Supper. They left that Upper Room and walked up the slope of the Mt. of Olives to a garden called Gethsemane. This was one of the places where olives were pressed. So, fitting. The greatest struggle in history occurred in that garden. Here, Jesus fought the battle, the result of which would seal His fate. Angels and devils awaited the outcome. The "press" in the garden took Him on to Golgotha.

The garden is not the place for the weak and vacillating. So often, we in the Christian faith are enamored with the beauty of the story. It is like a work of art to be hung and admired, a play to watch, or a shallow series that unfolds each Sunday morning. Christianity has its beauty. None other can compare. But, when one goes to the garden, it is not mountain-top, fuzzy feelings, it's the "press." The "health and wealth theology kids" are not even on the same page. Nor are those who shrink from the surrender and settle for a self-centered liberalism or legalism. The "celebration" we are hearing so much about in public worship services today may have little to do with a garden experience. Wrong models can do that. Gethsemane has its offense. Not everyone is willing to walk the narrow Gospel road, but it is the only path that leads to spiritual surrender. To follow Christ is to enter a lifestyle of suffering and that is not overly attractive to the shallow Christian. If one looks at the price for discipleship and it is too high, They put it down.

I Stand By The Door

Don't toy with it. Here in the garden the battle is either won or lost. Church members that play the game seldom, if ever, walk on to the garden. The game requires no suffering and has less strain. And, there's so much more company on that road.

Let's pull back the curtain and watch Jesus in Gethsemane. He knew the end was near, and He was the target of the religionists. It is almost always so. He had tried to prepare His disciples for the inevitable. But smooth roads are much easier to travel. His description of future events didn't coincide with their concept of a Messiah. They wanted, and expected, a warrior-conqueror, a political giant and genius that would eliminate their enemies, and lead them to world conquest.

As the disciples relaxed in the beautiful surroundings, Jesus went on a little farther. There, alone with His Father, the struggle began. He was human, as well as Divine. Earlier He had said, *I came to do the will of my Father.* The test was on. In His perfect wisdom, He knew what potentially faced Him. Now in what must be one of the most intimate dialogues between the Son and the Father, He said, *Father, if thou be willing, remove this cup from Me. (Luke 22:42)*

May we pause here? I do not in any way, understand the depth of these words. Only the Holy Trinity could fathom such a conversation. It had to do with the human, the Divine, and much more. At that moment He cried, *Isn't there another way?* The physical suffering, He was about to endure plumbs the depth of human pain and torment. Add to this the emotional stress. To die by crucifixion numbered Him with a common criminal – a rodent to be destroyed. It also carried with it the feeling of rejection by those who had been by His side for over three years.

Such a spectacle in death would bring reproach on His mother and family. With everyone watching. No wonder He asked, *Is there another way?*

Jesus was also Divine. He possessed every attribute of God the Father and God the Holy Spirit. Everything from eternity past pointed to this time and place. The Holy Trinity knew what they faced, and they would face it together. Everything they had to do with getting mankind to that better world climaxed here in the Garden. They had viewed the creation of the earth and its first resident, and said, *It is good.* But man was on probation. Caving into temptation, the first family surrendered everything that was good and holy for something they did not need in another Garden. Their sin necessitated a penalty, and it was death. *The soul that sinneth it shall die. (Ezekiel 18:4) The wages of sin is death. (Romans 6:23)* Divine justice confronted Divine love. A price must be paid, and it was the price of blood. *Without the shedding of blood, there is no remission for sin. (Hebrew 9:22)* The total sin of the human race was the mountain that must be moved. This ensued the sacrifice of countless animals down through the sin stained history of mankind, but they could not atone for sin. Someone must enter the stream of the human race and pay the price.

Enter Jesus! *But we see Jesus, who was made a little lower than the angels for the suffering of death, crowned with glory and honor; that He by the grace of God should taste death for every man. (Hebrews 2:9) Forasmuch then as the children are partakers of flesh and blood, He also Himself likewise took part of the same; that through death He might destroy him that had the power of death, that is, the devil. (Hebrews 2:14)* Jesus came to seek and to save the lost. In so doing, He suffered the penalty for sin. It was no game!

I Stand By The Door

No, I do not understand the depth of Jesus' words. But, let's look on. It wasn't just the incredible physical and emotional pain that Jesus shrank from. More importantly, because others had been put to death by crucifixion, He must taste the price for sin. He who had not sinned became our substitute that He might reconcile us to God. He who had never once disobeyed His Father must stand in the arena where all the forces of hell were gathered and feel the sting of the price for willful disobedience. The just for the unjust. The "cup" was the issue.

No one else ever walked this road. No one else could. Jesus left the splendor of heaven, walked away from a holy, angelic environment, and identified Himself with man. The "cup" was a bitter reminder of how the human race had fallen, and to what extent God would go to restore him. *Father, may this cup pass?* From the standpoint of His Divinity this was the battleground and the battle. At a point in time our Lord took the sins of Adam's race and paid the penalty. At the critical moment of His agony on the cross, He cried out, *Father, Father, why hast Thou forsaken Me?* Only a holy God could know the depth of this question. The Father could not look on sin. He turned and both the Father and the Son felt the pain that accompanied the price.

He, the Son, was bruised for our iniquities. With His stripes, we are healed. We owed the debt. He paid the price for us. How can a mere human understand?

We should be forever grateful that the Garden was not the end. The Trinity didn't go into a discussion of "what if?" It was settled before the foundation of the world. Jesus went on to utter words that reverberated through the corridors of hell and heaven.

They drove a nail deep into the heart of Satan and angelic choirs sang. What words? *Not my will, but Thine be done.* We heard a cry, *Let this cup pass.* Now we hear resolve, *Not my will, but Thine.* Without the cry, we are not serious enough to resolve. In the cry, we hear the sob in the heart that counts the cost. In the resolve, we get the confirmation of the alignment of the human will with God's. In the cry we have the soil that produces brokenness. Without brokenness we cannot enter the area of spirituality that produces holiness. Nor, can we see productive evangelism. Until we can look at the cost of following Christ, and say, *Not my will but Thine be done*, we are only playing the game.

Brokenness is an indispensable ingredient in evangelism. *They that sow in tears shall reap in joy. He that goeth forth and weepeth, bearing precious seed, shall doubtless come again, with rejoicing, bringing his sheaves with him. (Psalm 126:5-6)* William Booth, the great soulwinning founder of the Salvation Army said, "There is never a time when I cannot close my eyes and weep over the lost of the world." There must be a brokenness in evangelism. It is always from a "weeping heart" in Gethsemane to a death at Calvary. No garden, no cross. It is the natural order. To the heart of every fervent, Spirit-led soulwinner comes a confrontation with submission to God. We can turn and walk away. If not, "we enter the press" and experience brokenness.

Gethsemane always leads to a cross. Here we experience a death to self-centeredness and walk on to Pentecost. We then are endued with a power from another world, and it enables us to touch lost people. It is not a game - it is a garden!

I Stand By The Door

Something is unique about a Divine Enduement. It is not to be confused with what we may try to do in the flesh, but it does bring a positive approach to evangelism. Paul said, *I can do all things through Christ which strengthens me. (Philippians 4:13)* We can be positive because our sufficiency is of God. Our success is contingent upon total dependence on Him. He releases His power into us. He places the seed of perfect love in the soil of our heart. It germinates, grows, and produces a full-grown passion for the lost. We enjoy the high honor and privilege of success and it is all to the glory of God. God's surrendered soldiers are not failures or losers. We are co-laborers with Him.

Our Lord must be grieved to see His Church settle for so little. We can cloak our inadequacy in false humility, wallowing in an unhealthy sense of unworthiness to win souls. We'll not be alone. Our inadequacy can also be hidden in "a sophisticated approach to church." This is evidenced in a passive, tepid, approach to evangelism. Converts to Christ are won by "proxy" – through someone else. Worse yet – walk-ins. While this crowd would agree that we need to win the lost to Christ, they are "Mar's Hill Christians." They are always trying to find another way. They possess volumes on church growth principles and statistics. It's not unusual for them to travel to the ends of the earth to catch a morsel that falls from the table of some super-leader-Christian. They return home with glassy eyes and relate detail upon detail of some life-changing experience only to fall back into the same rut. This is only cloaking an inadequacy.

We tend to equate study and searching for doing. They're not equal. In the process we become professional students of evangelism – never soulwinners. Not yet. It's all a part of a game.

While we spend valuable time and a lot of money searching somewhere else, God calls us to a garden. It is low on prominence, but high on productivity.

In our quiet time we know it is a supernatural enduement we need, and it only comes after a brokenness in the garden. Without a Gethsemane, soulwinning is very difficult. With it, we become channels through which God pours out His love to a lost world. We are not the source or the power, but God uses us. In our weakness, we become strong. Our inadequacy is replaced with power born in the experience of submission. No other place or position is so fulfilling.

We may not agree on how, but most Christians would agree something must be done to reach the lost for Christ. But, soulwinning is not a viable part of the average Christian's lifestyle. Maybe it has to do with "the doctrine we practice." On paper, we believe we have the responsibility to make every unsaved person aware of Christ's claims. On paper, we believe that soul of every individual will live on somewhere in eternity. On paper, we believe we must be born again to reach heaven. On paper, we believe in a literal heaven and hell. On paper, we believe in eternal punishment for the unsaved. The gap between what we say we believe, and what we do, suggests the contemporary holiness Church have a glaring problem.

Ours is an "inherited doctrine." Doctrine on the printed page is not necessarily doctrine inscribed on human hearts. Inherited doctrine tends to become diluted. Only as it is re-born in each generation can it be personal, alive, and handed intact to the succeeding generation. If we know what should be done to reach lost people, why aren't we doing it?

I Stand By The Door

This is a question that is relevant to us. Our response will be handed to the next generation. Now, if you and your church are totally involved in evangelizing your community, please don't get exercised about what has been said. Keep it up. God bless you. However, not everyone is on your level.

The incentives for soulwinning are numerous. To not become involved ultimately carries a heavy penalty. Let me mention one that isn't on the top of the list for holiness people. <u>There is a judgement for believers</u>. *For we must all appear before the judgement seat of Christ.* (Romans 14:10, II Corinthians 5:10) Christians and non-Christians will face judgement. While it has not caught on in the church, our works will be judged. *The Lord shall judge <u>His</u> people.* (Hebrews 10:31) *It is a fearful thing to fall into the hands of the living God.* (Hebrews 30:31) Note these verses are together. Lost somewhere in the practiced translation of our doctrine from one generation to another is the issue of judgement for the believer. It needs to be taken off the shelf and owned by us today.

Perhaps this is due to an erroneous interpretation of salvation by faith alone. We do not wish to be "salvation by works" people. Salvation is by faith, but the Bible says, *Faith without works is dead, being alone.* (James 2:17) *What does it profit, my brethren, though a man say he has faith, and have not works? Can faith (that faith) save him?* (James 2:14)

How convenient it is to ignore evangelism in order not to appear we are working our way to heaven. Not to worry! We are a million miles from it. When it comes to works as they relate to evangelism, there is not enough evidence to convict us. But what if we really will be judged?

Listen to Paul, *For we must appear before the judgement seat of Christ. Knowing therefore the terror of the Lord, we persuade men. (II Corinthians 5:10-11)* We would do well to study the consequences of willful disobedience. Imagine standing before God in judgement. That alone should bring us to a sobering reality. This is not a game. No place for acting or rationalizing. We will face our works and motives, stripped of every excuse. We will see if what we <u>say and do</u> square with the Book. A paraphrased translation of II Corinthians 5:10-11, reads, *For we must all stand before Christ to be judged and have our lives laid bare before Him. Each of us will receive whatever he deserves for the good or bad things he has done in his earthly life. It is because of this solemn fear of the Lord, which is ever present in our minds, that we work so hard to win others.*

For so long, we have ignored the importance of the fear of God in evangelism. Worse – we get an "A" for it. However, fear, reverent fear, is an authentic incentive in soulwinning. We may now have a generation that in reality has no fear of a holy, all-powerful God. This has to be taught and modeled. We have overdosed on God's love. I wonder if it is understood at all.

However much God loves us is how much He hates sin. To presume on God's goodness and mercy is a tragic mistake. In our minds He has become a benevolent father image with nothing to do but heed our every call. Familiarity at times is a blessing, but when it comes to God, it can engender carelessness and little respect. He does not settle for this.

Imagine a frown from God! He has placed world evangelization in the hands of His Church. He made no other plans. To assume that He smiles when millions have never heard about His Son is unreal.

I Stand By The Door

To believe He is pleased when His Church is not totally involved in soulwinning is not being intellectually honest. Believers will be judged. Try to fathom what it would be like to stand before God, have the records read, and have Him look at us with a frown. Displeased and hurt, without even a word, the look on His face would sting more than anything else that has happened to us. Our one desire at that moment will be to please Him. Nothing else will matter. Whatever kept us from reaching the lost in life will not have been worth it. Holiness people need to receive a fresh revelation of judgement for believers.

I listened to one of the nation's prominent church leaders recently. He was critical of other preachers and laymen for using fear as an incentive to get people saved. He is not alone. I have thought and prayed a lot about this. I have reached a conclusion. Without it, Old Testament prophet's voices would probably never been heard. They spoke of judgement and the wrath of God. They cried out and at times used unorthodox methods. Those they were trying to save hated them. But they continued. Their call was to return to God or suffer bitter persecution. Some were put to death for the words they brought. I must believe they obeyed and honored God. Despite what is being said today about evangelism, fear can be an incentive to win souls.

In the New Testament, John the Baptist spoke about judgement. He called for people to repent, turn to God, or be lost. Jesus must have been pleased, because He said, *no one was greater than John.* He was called the forerunner of Christ the Messiah. Fear was used as an incentive for people to get right with God. The same theme is laced throughout the New Testament. My point? You just can't buy into everything that is being said and written on how to evangelize.

Before you go off the cliff, may I say fear can be used the wrong way. Like any other method. But my friend, there is no wrong way to get someone saved.

Sinners do not always fit into the little standard boxes we insist on putting them in. I have a fear we have made soulwinning a science. Special compartments for each personality. We may know so much that we have really given up on getting men and women to God. Spiritual reproduction may well have been replaced with a scientific study of culture and psychology. This is great for conversation but requires no commitment or positive results. We should obviously study culture and know a little about psychology. But, for the sake of lost souls, let us leave the board and classrooms and get to the people.

When one hasn't experienced the brokenness that a Gethsemane experience produces, he must settle for the mundane. There is nothing left to do but compile statistics and waste hours in a non-productive whatever. We are talking about it, but it doesn't get many to God. Not so with the broken. The heart that has thought and prayed its way through the "press" cannot settle for anything less than a burning heart for evangelism. It is the *"meat to eat"* that much of the floundering church knows little about. "It's the fire shut up in our bones, and we cannot stay."

David Brainerd, evangelist to the American Indians, wrote, "I care not how or where I live, or what hardship I go through, so that I can but gain souls." His surrender to Christ led him to an early death, but he left his mark on our world. R. G. Flexon, one of the greatest soulwinners produced by the holiness movement said, "Every day of my life is taken up with a consuming desire to see the lost saved."

I Stand By The Door

He was the most effective evangelist I used when pastoring. He was the ultimate personification of combining personal and public evangelism. George Whitfield wrote, "When the church loves compassion, Christianity confines itself to acts of worship, but when it is filled with love for a needy world it grows from worship to activity. This is the hour for action. We must take the offensive. We must mobilize an all-out crusade to win the lost. This is one task from which no Christian should consider himself exempt. Soulwinning is every Christian's job. John Wesley wrote, "Give me a hundred men who love God with all their hearts, and fear nothing but sin, and I will move the world." He told his preachers, "You have nothing to do but win souls." He would not be in synch with that church today. Sam Shoemaker said, "All vital movements make converters out of their converts."

The words of these great leaders jerk us back to reality. The message that must be preached is not about an easy way. We have tried that. It hasn't worked. What we need to say is not what the average man on the street, or next door, wants to hear. The "be good and you'll be happy" flies in the face of authentic Christianity.

We have insulted the intelligence of the very people we want to reach. In every field except contemporary Christianity, victories are only won through discipline and hardship. The world is cognizant of this. Down deep, under the crust, mankind is looking for a serious challenge spiritually. They do not need chaff! We have fallen all over them to give a message we think they want to hear, but it hasn't produced many "garden Christians." Their presence in our church on Sunday morning has fed the human ego but comes short of leading them to the place of complete surrender to God.

So, they walk away from church with the same hunger they arrived with, and a lot more confused about what really matters in life. We wonder why they aren't committed and schedule another meeting to analyze more statistics. We have only succeeded in adding "more players in the game," but few who go to the "garden." The Kingdom suffers. We "refine the cheerleading", but the lost are still lost.

May we one more time watch Jesus in Gethsemane? His crucial battle was won there. Every military leader realizes the moment the battle is either won or lost. It is a defining moment! So, it is in our battle with complete surrender to God. No tears, no triumph! No brokenness, no blessing! The secret of true spiritual growth is the "lost life", lost in Christ. In the garden we, in effect, lose our life in order to find it. It is the price for spiritual success. We spend ourselves rather than save ourselves. It is not preserving or hiding but losing and abandoning. It is giving up!

In our Gethsemane experience we kneel humbly, and look into the sweaty, tortured, tear-stained face of Jesus Christ. We watch as his sweat, like drops of blood, fall to the ground. Then His cry, *Father, if it is possible, let this cup pass from Me.* Every muscle and nerve in His body feels the pressure of the moment. Scenes, like a cinema, flash across His mind. Scenes of suffering humanity. Scenes of what He faced. Heaven and hell met head on! Everything settled in the area of His will. To go on meant the Cross, and the dreaded "cup." To stop now meant humanity forever lost without hope. Watch as He stiffens – views fallen man, so defiled, and in tears, broken, looks up to His Father, and said, "I'll do it!" *Not my will but Thine be done.*

That, my friend, is what God calls us to. Whatever hinders us from a complete surrender is a deadly enemy of that which is holy. However, it is wrapped. In the garden, what is good can be the foe of the very thing God designs for us. The practical can thwart life's best. Busyness can deter us from the road that leads to submission. The garden is a showcase of the battle for the human will. It is a battle that will lead to a death if we follow Christ's pattern.

It is true that Paul mentioned "a living sacrifice." *I beseech you therefore brethren, by the mercies of God, that you present your bodies, a living sacrifice, holy, acceptable unto God, which is your reasonable service.* (Romans 12:1) But, only after we receive the product of His sacrifice can we become a living sacrifice to God. Paul also wrote, *Yield yourselves unto God, as those that are alive from the dead, and your members as instruments of righteousness unto God.* (Romans 6:13) The sacrifice has to be slain before it can be offered, used, and come alive. No one who has ever bowed in total submission to God have left fussing, screaming, and resisting on to a cross. The sacrifice has to die, but through its death it will come alive and reproduce in the life of another.

I've always been fascinated with the early church. There is a holy something, a divine ingredient, a resistless, super-natural energy that called and led those New Testament saints. They were impassioned and empowered. Whatever it is they had; we obviously need today if we "have a prayer" in impacting our culture. Sorry, but the world isn't impressed with what we are doing. This should not surprise us when, according to statistics, there is not all that much difference in how we live in and outside the church.

I Stand By The Door

This was not true in the first-generation church. Someone has said, "the culture is a reflection of the church in every generation." I hope not from what I see. However, God is calling His church to pour itself into the mix of our world and change it. This will not happen unless we go to the garden.

The garden doesn't insure a large church, fame, or approval. Nor does it necessarily mean financial security and good health. One may be ridiculed for such a dramatic allegiance to God. Enthusiasm may be misunderstood. Plans may be rejected and a vision to reach lost people criticized. Carnality hates the holy, so resentment could come. Foes may well be those of our own household. Our closest friends may leave. But when it is settled in the garden, we can make it. And, by saying, "Not my will but God's," such a release will come! If necessary, we will walk away from the crowd. We have heard something we shall never forget – the sound of spiritual victory. Bring on the cross! And Pentecost! Our life can never be the same. Once you have been there, nothing else compares.

Friend, I appeal to you in Jesus' name. Out there, they await us. Walking in darkness, afraid, bound, confused, lost people. They instinctively sense there must be a place of release, a door somewhere to get to God. I have to believe our own heart throbs as we revel in God's grace. We are so used to the warmth of His love. Yet, our heart must be pricked and hurt. If it not for God's love and His providence we would be one of them outside, thirsty, afraid, lost, doomed to die for our sins. But, one day someone told us about Jesus. In a moment, He changed us. If we fail to share Him now, how can we face Him?

I Stand By The Door

How can we stand in His presence and know we did not tell the lost about His love? Why would we expect to spend eternity with Him?

If our plan involves travelling to the garden one day, we must do it now. Waiting to fully surrender to God's perfect will only hardens our heart. Only by surrender can we experience a heart broken over lost people. The Breath of Evangelism is now being felt around the world. We must be in the place and state of mind to catch the current. It is from the very heart of God. It can carry us into the regions of the lost. Our Lord wants to pour us into Satan's stronghold to snatch precious souls, and carry them, like lambs, safely home.

This is our task and assignment. Our charge and commission! If I am convinced of anything, it is that holiness people need a Gethsemane. Nothing short of "giving up" can change cold, calloused, hearts. I have a fear we have adopted questionable models. I find no pleasure in saying this, but I humbly ask you to think about it. We have, in desperation, nearly read ourselves into spiritual insanity. We have traveled to seminars and conferences until we are numb. We have learned the language of "church correctness." We are more versed in psychology and human techniques than the supernatural. We are more peer-driven than we are prayer-driven. But, when we have run our course, and wore ourselves out, we will one day have to let it all go and admit church growth is the natural result of a truly yielded heart to God.

If you are playing the game, enjoy now. If you have gone to the garden, hang on, it is a wonderful ride. And, the best is yet to come!

I Stand By The Door

I Stand By The Door

THE BRIDGE
Part One

Words such as tomorrow, future and eternity, raise a wide range of responses today. Everything from excitement and hope to fear, dread and anxiety. A lot of it depends where you are in "the here and now." Circumstances often dictate what we think and do. But, in a broader sense, people from every segment of our society feel that something of major proportion is on the horizon. It is an intangible. A general uneasiness seems to prevail. The political scene in Washington and the closing out of a century no doubt contributes to this. Few people are satisfied with the "sound bite" assurances of the politicians. Nor are they certain about the economy. Add to this the decline in morals in what is now referred as a post-Christian era, one could hardly be surprised at the mood in America.

Life itself is fragile and uncertain. None of us has a clue as to what a day will bring. We are admonished on the one hand to get swallowed up in the positive thinking philosophy and on the other descend into a state of panic. Somewhere in between I believe we can find the answers we need. There must be a rational something that we can hold on to as storms lash against what we believed were sure foundations. Our time calls for a firm grip on eternal issues. Without this, the prospects for the future are not overly attractive.

At the risk of sounding trite, we, with God's grace and strength, can face tomorrow. It may not be easy.

I Stand By The Door

We can face the future because we know some things in advance. In a day when some "only know they do not know", the child of God knows! When we go to prayer in Christ's name, we invite God to bring His resources to unite with ours. Under His direction we can be confident and endure.

We first have anchorage to the past. Important? It is vital to emotional and spiritual security. We cannot, or at least should not, live in the past. It is non-productive – often crippling. Yet, our security for the future must originate in someone or something that can bridge eternity future with eternity past. Only God qualifies.

It is a consolation to reach into the past and find our roots in the words, *In the beginning God created the heavens and the earth.* God liked what He saw and said, *Let us make man in our image – after our likeness, male and female created He them.* At a point in time, we began. We are not the result of some cosmic explosion or purposeless cause. Mankind was formed by the Master Creator. His breath made man a living soul.

Charles Darwin, the father of the theory of evolution, eventually found his way back to God. When asked his favorite topic – just prior to his death, he replied, "Christ Jesus and His salvation." The theory of evolution played out in his heart and mind and came up short. He needed an anchor to his past. Only a Creator God could provide such security. We have a firm anchor to the past.

We also have an anchor for the present. Because of what was, we can get a good grip on the issues that matter today.

I Stand By The Door

Since an eternal God is our bridge from eternity future with eternity past, our anchor is held firmly in the present age. What a comforting thought. The "signs of the time" are in evidence all around us. Technology is unfolding at an incredible rate of speed. Alvin Taffler's book, "Future Shock" is now nearly archaic. In less time than it took a few decades ago to travel to and from town for supplies, one can travel from the United States to Europe. Travel has increased. Community landscapes are rapidly changing as building is now going on at an unprecedented rate. These and numerous other signs of the time could cause us to panic.

But the God that provides an anchor to our past is here now to comfort our hearts. He has permitted mankind to unlock secrets of the universe that have been there since the beginning of time. Though some may question even His very existence, He is in control. Nothing can happen to us out of His permissive will. Storms may come. Only He knows how much His children will be tried but take heart. The one that controls the universe comes to us daily with words such as, *Fear not, for I am with you. Don't be dismayed, for I am your God. I will strengthen you, I will help you, I will uphold you with my right hand.* (Isaiah 41:10) Our anchor is firm today.

But what about the future? Someone says, "I can't be concerned about that, I'm trying to survive today." Be assured, tomorrow will probably come. And then what? If the past and present are any indication as to what the future holds, we will need an anchor.

It is good to remind ourselves that we do not have to live tomorrow today. When it comes, He will be there.

I Stand By The Door

A common remark heard today is "the future is now." Not quite. That is like saying the night is day. It is a plus that none of us know what the future holds, but we will make it. The supernatural God that created this amazing universe will be there tomorrow. This is not fantasy stuff. It is more than hope. Hope is good – but this goes farther. It is a promise! It is reality today. That is the anchor and it is fastened to the Rock. The only way we cannot make it is if He fails. That is not a possibility. The one that can reach back into the long ago – before anything was, as we know it – can also reach into eternity future. Both are in His hands, and these mighty creative hands touch ours and He says, *When you pass thru threatening waters, I'll be with you, and thru the deepest rivers, you'll not go under. When you walk thru the most intense trials of fire, you'll not be burned. Neither will the flames of affliction feed on you.*

Take comfort child if you know Him. When the news frightens, and when the word comes that would sweep you under – Hold on! When you lack for a friend and they are not there, do not despair. When Satan laughs amid chaos and calamity, look up. When foundations shake and what you've held onto crumbles and you're left with empty hands, Hold on! His is a firm grip. Do not let go! The One who kept you yesterday, and walks with you today, will carry you tomorrow if necessary. His age-old plan is to get you to that better land. He will!

THE BRIDGE
Part Two

Jerusalem to Emmaus was only seven miles. But they were long miles that day for Cleopas and his friend. They had watched in disbelief as an exciting plan for their future came unraveled. What started out in their minds as a dream of release from Roman rule ended in disaster. Their Master and leader was put to death by crucifixion like a common criminal. Hope for a new day was dashed. The whole senseless scheme of events had plunged them into deep despair.

Three miserable days had come and gone since their world came crashing down around them. Theirs were lofty plans. Now they were over – gone! Once they brightened their days and comforted them during long nights. Now it is history! Their prayers were for such a Deliverer. He came, but all of it ended in a cruel senseless death. How could it have happened? Change shook their world. Questions raced through their minds, but answers were elusive. They were just going home. What else?

Emmaus was now close by. They were nearly home. The sun was sinking fast in the west. How tired they were from the ugly events and their seven-mile journey. Events of the past week played out in their minds. All at once another traveler joined them and inquired about something he heard them say. Not recognizing that it was Jesus, they asked in amazement, *Haven't you heard? If not, you must be the only one who doesn't know."* (Luke 24:18)

I Stand By The Door

Then came a sad commentary about their leader and His death. Oh, they had heard about some woman who had visited His tomb. But the word is, "He's gone." To further complicate the whole matter, we are told some angels said, "*He's alive.*" It makes no sense. For centuries, prayers had gone up to God for a Messiah to come. We believed He was the One. Now He is gone! But, <u>we trusted</u> *that He was the One who would redeem Israel. (Luke 24:21)* He was our last hope. Not now. Then Jesus spoke to them and they knew Him.

The words, "*But we trusted*" have echoed and re-echoed in countless lives across the years. Change is inevitable, but it is often the enemy of peace. It invades us all, and it can interrupt. Ours is a changing world. The best of us occasionally long for something or someone that is changeless. The spiraling value of antiques is proof of this. What our forefathers considered trash has become our treasures. We are repelled at the idea of not keeping pace with our neighbors in technology, yet spend hard-earned cash for something that ties us to the past. Almost anything! This is evidence that change is not always exactly what we want. It was not for the two Emmaus bound travelers.

"*But we trusted!*" Been there? And, "to see the things shaken that can be shaken to produce what cannot be shaken" is of little consolation at the time. Let's be honest. Buried deep in the human psyche is an occasional longing for escape from change. Especially when it comes to the unpleasant.

The "blessing in disguise thing" is not what we want to hear about when unwelcome change rumbles across our world.

I Stand By The Door

The world has caved in on many people today. The sky is not falling yet, but to some, it's close. They are encountering storms that make them feel they are left twisting in the wind.

Clichés and stock answers are worthless at such times. When the physician says, "The prognosis is not good, make preparations", it's not easy. When one walks to the cemetery with a spouse, life will never be the same. A child overhears a conversation about an unfaithful parent, home will never be home again. A parent watches a dear child turn their back on everything they have been taught, and walk a path that will lead to destruction, and their heart breaks.

When after years of sacrifice and hard work, a business fails, and a family is headed for possible bankruptcy and disgrace. What do they do? The phone rings. A horrible accident has changed forever the life of dear friends. A treasured relationship is shattered. Hearts broken. Families and friendships are strained. In these, and so many other circumstances, we long for rest, stability, and understanding. We desperately want things to return to what they one-time were.

There is hope! We cannot roll back the clock. Sometimes I could wish it were possible. But, look in the shadows of the storm. The winds are still blowing, and it is dark all around. Maybe you can't see Him, but Jesus is present. And, He doesn't change! He can help!

"Change and decay all around I see,
O Thou Who changest not, abide with me."

I Stand By The Door

We are in the cycle of change and we cannot get out or off. Nature, nations, fashions, families and friends change. But there is One who is changeless. Unlike so many leaders today, He is <u>unchangeable in His character</u>. Even fickle Pilate had to say, "I find no fault in Him." We long for leaders that are not "poll driven", but credible. And, also for a populace that values integrity over an all-time high of the Dow stock market exchange. Jesus qualifies. He never changes in who He is regardless of the pressure. We can rest in that today. His word is true and will be true when our little world is being tossed by the cold winds of life. He is honorable. He is honest and not swayed by public opinion. He can be counted on. Lean on Him.

<u>Jesus never changes in His love</u>. His is a great and universal love. He not only says He loves us, He proved it at Calvary. *Greater love hath no man than this, that a man lay down his life for a friend. (John 15:13)* He did this, but He went the second mile, He even died for His enemies. To you who have suffered the loss of love from a spouse or trusted friend, look to Jesus. In good and bad days, His love is constant. When we turn our backs on Him, He still loves us. When others walk away, He stays. When you're rejected, and sit alone, He's there. When you feel so unworthy, and all of us are, His love will warm and heal your heart. When you cannot communicate your deepest feelings, and you want to, He understands. Relax in His love. If you have sinned, messed up with everything and everyone, and want to change, tell Him. He loves and forgives. His love never changes.

<u>Jesus never changes in His purpose for us</u>. *He came to seek and to save that which was lost. (Matthew 18:11)* At Calvary He bridged the deep chasm that separated sinful man from a holy God. The penalty for sin is death.

I Stand By The Door

On the Cross He raised one hand up to the Father, and with the other reached down to us. He paid the price. What the blood of countless animal sacrifices could not do, He did! Once for all – for all time. His purpose is to clean us up from sin's filth, put us on the right road, and get us to heaven. He never changes.

Cleopas and his friend made an interesting remark about their encounter with Jesus. *Did not our hearts burn within us as He walked with us and opened the scriptures? (Luke 24:32)* No doubt, many questions were still unanswered, but His presence was enough. He went home with them and shared a meal. He will with us.

Theirs too was a changing world. Really! Yet, He came and warmed their hearts. Something new began for them that day. They started the re-building of their world. Whatever future life dealt them, they could never question what happened when Jesus walked and talked with them. They could hardly wait to return to Jerusalem and share their experience with their friends.

Jesus still walks the road of human life. He will warm the heart of anyone that can work their way through the fog of whatever is happening. He is there, and He does not change. Has He appeared to you lately? If so, it might be helpful if you shared it with another traveler.

I Stand By The Door

THE TYRANNY OF TOLERANCE

A News report stated, "fourteen are dead, and eleven wounded. Littleton, Colorado has gone from a quiet, upscale community to a front-page story." Columbine High School, a place where it was not supposed to happen, is the latest and worst in a series of campus bloodbaths. From educators to politicians, answers are sought for such demonstration of hatred and violence. Preachers and social workers are bombarded with questions as to how and why such carnage could occur in civilized America. Television and radio talk-show people are interviewing leaders and sharing their own opinion. Once again, the law enforcement personnel are under terrific pressure and scrutiny to unravel the twisted details of this tragic event.

In Washington and state capitals, lawmakers are delegating the passage of additional regulations in hope that the violence can be curbed. Elected officials are rushing to microphones to make some kind of statement. One only refutes or echoes another. One prevailing cry is to spend more money, and/or, add another department of government, to serve as a cure-all for what is wrong. So, if everyone is under more strict control then that part of the population that break laws will somehow become good citizens. In a not so subtle way this is only the exploitation of a situation that is national in scope to advance a political agenda. History reveals the futility of such a philosophy.

Morality cannot be legislated. Every attempt in past cultures has produced the "tyranny of tolerance."

I Stand By The Door

Why? When morality is no longer a virtue to be cultivated in a society, eventually pseudo-morality will be imposed on the population through layer upon layer of laws. It is in effect handed down. When there is no Biblical authority recognized, then something must be in place to handle the inevitable hatred and hostility. If God is no longer at the center, man will be, and he cannot be predicted or trusted. In such an arrangement any attempt to promote morality and conscience will be met with an iron fist, or intolerance, and another kind of tolerance is born. The result? No concept of right and wrong. That is decided by each person.

A "tyranny of tolerance" is born when tolerance is carried to the extreme. It crushed any form of intolerance on the part of the populace. To stand against evil as defined by the Holy Scriptures is to face immediate opposition today. A nation, void of the Bible as the ruling authority, has set the stage for violence and anarchy. The surprise is that we are surprised when a Littleton, Colorado event occurs.

Few things remain the same in our world. Words undergo change in their meaning. Much of this has to do with a cultural shift that influences the moral climate. As an example, the word conscience has undergone a radical change. At one time it was defined as "a knowledge or feeling of right and wrong, with a compulsion to do right; moral judgement that prohibits or opposes the violation of a previously recognized ethical principle."

Note a more recent definition: "conformity to <u>one's own sense of right conduct</u>." To each his own. Under this definition, there is no absolute standard.

I Stand By The Door

Our youth have been methodically and deliberately made to conform or to become politically incorrect. To take a position that God places within us a conscience to guide us toward righteousness is met with hostility in educational classrooms and courtrooms. First, God has been ruled off limits to such places. Second, if He does exist, He has no authority to say what is right or wrong. Third, no one is to take issue with anyone when it comes to morals, in almost any situation. The Bible is no longer relevant, nor is God our judge. Each of us act according to what we think is right. It is tolerance bent and twisted. From such a philosophy evolves eventually the "tyranny of tolerance." It is tolerance out of control. This leads to unbridled license. Even license to kill and destroy. "When there is no King in Israel, everyone does what is right in his own eyes." When there are no moral absolutes and no moral authority we are without a foundation and common direction.

After reviewing the cruel and cowardly killings, our national leaders encourage citizens to respond with words not violence. At the same time, they order bombs to drop on a sovereign nation in another part of the world. Day after day, the carnage continues. Television viewers, young and old, are witnessing death and suffering. Collateral damage (meaning civilian casualties) is explained away with amazing skill. It is not my intention to judge if one should or should not be involved militarily. (I do have my opinion) However, when observing how we respond as a nation, our youth must believe it all borders on insanity and inconsistency. Respond with words? We have created a monster in America. We can't live with it, nor do we have the moral fiber to let it die. When we listen to the count of the dead in our war in Kosovo, we don't miss a step on Wall Street. In fact, the war has sent the Dow Jones into orbit.

I Stand By The Door

Dead people in another part of the world doesn't register with Main Street America. We no longer know right from wrong. In fact, who is to say there is a right and wrong? It is relative and I'll decide!

The "tyranny of tolerance" has taken us to where we are today. If it feels good, do it! We have been liberated from the rules. No longer can one say something is wrong, even if it adversely affects another. From homes and families to government, our lives have been changed. Everything we do is the result of someone or something else anyway. Who accepts responsibilities for their actions? We have witnessed tolerance taken to the extreme, and the harvest is not quite what we wanted. It should have been expected. The law of seedtime and harvest is still in operation. God's laws can be disobeyed, but they cannot be broken.

We have had an aggressive upward mobility in America, and as a people, we have taken full credit for it. We've forgotten that it is God that gives the power to gain in wealth. In this process, we have ignored His laws and bulldozed a couple of generations over the cliff. They have missed an all-important principle, how to discern the difference between right and wrong. From what they've been taught and seen modeled, there is no absolute standard. Even in the prison population, I'm told the older, seasoned inmates dread to live with the young. They fear them because they do not sense or recognize right and wrong. Try to imagine what is happening on the streets, in the houses, and in the schools of our nation, and you have a view of reality.

"What is there about the word no that you don't understand?" is now more a joke than a serious question.

I Stand By The Door

Let me re-word the question. "What is there about the word 'no' that keeps us from using it?" Answer. Tolerance carried to the extreme. This brand of tolerance becomes a tyrant, not a virtue to be desired. When those in authority no longer say "no" it is a disservice to those involved. This, in many cases, is to hope that someone will just go away. In others it is a philosophy born out of a hostility to an authority figure in their own lives that is now reproducing. For yet others, it is a radical failure to assume the responsibility to discipline under the guise of love. It's not love, it's saying in effect, I want you to be happy, do what pleases you. They do, and we cannot understand when a school becomes killing fields and war zones for our kids.

Tolerance is a good word. So is freedom, when used in the right context. But when pushed beyond the point of reason, they become negative. We have stretched tolerance to the ridiculous in our country when it comes to moral responsibility. This is not only an indictment of society, but of the church. Little wonder we have so little impact on our culture. Tolerance can mean freedom from bigotry, but also permissiveness. It can mean to endure, but also the amount of variation allowed from a standard or accuracy. In the name of piety and maturity, we have permitted a dilution of biblical-based righteousness. In the name of love, or being all things to all people, we have allowed, or tolerated, a variation from doctrinal purity. As a result, the church, which should be providing a moral compass for our culture, is lost sailing in a sea without a rudder.

I'm sure there is enough blame to go around for a Littleton, Colorado tragedy. As a nation, we have stretched tolerance until we have no moral standards.

I Stand By The Door

We have also surrendered freedom without scarcely a whimper. The Church has emphasized tolerance until we are much more a homogenized blob than a body of believers with distinctive. And, we've had a cheering section that calls for more of the same. We're now in a "me too mode" until our message offends none, justifies everyone, and grieves God. In a frantic effort to make people feel good about themselves, we have blurred the lines of the new birth and Christlikeness.

Families have pushed tolerance until we are hard pressed to define authentic parent and child roles. The education system of our land has all but surrendered to the students. Much of this is caused by a deep, parental problem, and a national political agenda that has crowded God out of the equation. Can we be intellectually honest and be surprised at the anger and hostility on school campuses? With children brought up on a diet of no moral standards and absolutes, what could we honestly expect? We are reaping the harvest of the tyranny of tolerance and we have only witnessed the tip of the iceberg.

Only a moral revolution can change our culture. Educators are probably not ready for it. The politicians enacting more laws is only an exercise in futility. The polls are not conclusive. The judicial system is mostly pompous and arrogant, out of touch with biblical morality themselves. God, in some way, must be brought back to the center of homes and families. A new, but old, set of values must be adopted by parents. Television and the movie industry have shaped us. It won't change. It's the money. The media is no longer a communicator of news as much as it is the message. The economy has eclipsed eternity in our warped sense of values. Money is more important than morality.

I Stand By The Door

In this moral revolution, the Church, if it is to be a factor, will have to move from a vague, bland, concept of religion to Christian discipleship. The unanswerable defense of Christianity is still a Christ-like person. Anything less will not penetrate the spiritual darkness that blankets our country today. The only tested antidote to what causes a massacre on school grounds is a deliberate move to a restoration of morality. Character does matter. Believe it! The tyranny of tolerance has produced anarchy. Tolerance, unbridled, becomes a tyrant that destroys what is good and righteous. What is left is really intolerance. When tolerance reigns, immorality results. The absence of a moral absolute produces a vacuum. What rushes to fill it are hostility, anger and violence.

We are well aware of what we don't believe. Just look around – in homes, schools and streets. What is needed is an articulation of what we do believe. Are there things worth dying for? Do we have a set of standards, from which we will not move? How far in the wrong direction are we willing to go? Are there moral absolutes that we will not surrender or compromise? In our home? Business? Career? Recreation? Entertainment? Are we willing to measure our values with the Bible? Is there a defined off-limits? Even under pressure or attack?

If not, we are controlled by the tyranny of tolerance and unable to be a player in the spiritual restoration of our culture. The situation is not hopeless. Thank God. *If my people, which are called by my name, will humble themselves and pray, seek my face, and turn from their wicked way, then I will hear their prayer, I will forgive their sin, and heal their land."* (II Chronicles 7:14)

I Stand By The Door

We've been under a subtle form of tyranny and are dominated by it more than we think. The only solution? Christlikeness. And it has its price.

BEYOND FORGIVENESS?

Is he beyond forgiveness? Before you get spiritual and give a neat answer, so peculiar to the saved, please hear me out. I watched him walk away. I'll never forget him. Many that I've known better and longer impressed me less. His eyes told a sad despicable story of neglect and desertion at a critical time in his life. I didn't detect bitterness, although he's entitled to it, given his experiences. He was unloved and worse, unwanted, by the very people that could have helped him most. In a cruel turn of events, he watched his home come apart. His parents took off in different directions. No one wanted him, so he grew up tossing from one foster home to another. Now, he's a man with unbelievable scars, and has no clue as to how to smooth out the rumble strips on the road ahead.

He's honest and hardworking. You can trust him. His one overarching desire is to be a good husband and father to his young children. He'll never have an easy life. Too many things against him. He struggles daily to crowd out the memory of his past, but you can't miss it. His face paints a picture. Hurt. Rejection. Passion. Occasional tenderness. Even though life's tough, he longs to trust others, and lives with the hope that people will trust him. One side of him is tough and calloused, ready to face anyone anywhere. He's street-smart. The other side is the one I'll never forget. The crushed boy with dreams like others, and a hurt so deep, has now become a man. He's reaching out for attention and acceptance from someone. Anyone! Where will it all end? Is he beyond forgiveness? Because of a total lack of understanding?

I Stand By The Door

He has no concept of spiritual reality and has never seriously considered that God could love him.

I didn't believe it earlier, but some people are void of the basic knowledge of how much God wants to forgive and love them. What little love, if any, they've felt has ended in heartache. It's a life without the Bible and the church. One generation can descend into total ignorance of a loving God due to carelessness on the part of those responsible. Is there a way to change this man? Again, no "canned answers." Is he beyond forgiveness? In his mind? Or, has he ever thought about it? If spiritual things are spiritually discerned and he has no sense of discernment, where is he? Whatever the answer, it has to do in part with what has happened in our country. Modern America has lost its consciousness of God, and the importance of this transcends family planning, healthy self-esteem, retirement seminars, and a soaring, out of control stock market. This man is one of the many victims of our society. The price for ignoring God by wicked leaders and judges is beyond calculation. And, we're too intoxicated on the wine of our successes to fathom the depth of our moral decline. A popular political slogan, It's the economy stupid! No, you poor thing, it's eternity! Contrary to poll points we're skidding there as a nation. When families and homes are not built with the fabric of commitment and responsibility, the garment that protects the new generation is gaped open. What is exposed is a bleeding, hurting, and deeply scarred segment of our population. Our response? "I'm OK. You're OK." Maybe they'll just go away. God bless America! No, friend, no! They're here.

They'll be around. The jury is still out, but all of us, in one way or another, will pay the toll.

Is he beyond forgiveness? Church say it. We know it so well. No one is beyond the reach of God's forgiveness. Really? God is loving. He loves us all. "Red and yellow, black and white, we are precious in His sight." On and on it goes. We know John 3:16, so that settles it. We're home free. We're in! We love to testify to it as we converse with one another. It's a virtual testimony contest to see who has been saved the longest and best. It's great! I enjoy it. The war stories of how far down God had to reach to get us are legion and often heard by those that have a story they can't wait to relate. Again. It's a merry-go-round thing we do, and I suppose it's better than doing nothing. However, the witness seldom hits the street. People like this man will probably never catch the merry-go-round. He can't find it, and if he did, outside of a powerful manifestation of the Spirit, it would be meaningless to him. He's confused enough.

It's partially up to Christians to decide if this man is beyond forgiveness. His family isn't involved. When he was eleven, and in a foster home, he did attend Sunday School for a few months. In one of our own local churches. But he was soon transferred away. That is the sum total of his religious education. He talked about it. A great-grandmother was a member of a sister holiness denominational church. He never knew her.

Is he beyond forgiveness? Because the church has failed him. Wait, please don't get defensive. Are we deliberately in business to enlighten those in spiritual darkness? Here in America? Or, is there a vast segment of our nation's population outside? We will never say it, but what are the facts? Numerous congregations add no new members by profession of faith annually. Even after spending large amounts of funds.

I Stand By The Door

With no apparent accountability. I have to question the fairness of it all. When families outside the church feel little spiritual responsibility for the young, and the church is pre-occupied with an endless schedule of activities to feed itself, what happens to this man? When people old enough to be grandparents are still trying to find out who they are, what happens? If the church continues the crippling process of expending finances, time and energy upon itself, at the exclusion of reaching lost people, some are even now beyond forgiveness.

Satan is pleased with things as they are. Families are in trouble. Too many Christians are "fighting brush fires" about things that won't matter in eternity. Satan exploits the situation. While Christendom soars in meaningless religious oratory, souls live and die outside. While we fuss over service and worship style, and this in itself is evidence that our motor shut off somewhere, Satan doesn't care. He loves the "brush fires", for they hide the burning inferno that is destroying lives. He just claims more redeemable souls and they walk into eternity unforgiven.

Maybe there is a more personal something that is unfolding in this drama. For you and me, the possibility is sobering. Who are the unforgiven? Obviously, the lost, the untold. But some others may be blending in. Who? Enlightened, discipled, gifted, trained, professing Christians who refuse to evangelize lost people. Perhaps two groups are beyond forgiveness. They're poles apart, but on the same road.

Their destiny is identical, but they are not equal. If we know what to do, and it's God's will, and we fail to obey, we may well be beyond forgiveness.

I Stand By The Door

Please watch the process as it marches toward judgement and eternity. Two lives that differ in a thousand ways but meshing together as time meets eternity. If I had to make a choice, I would rather face God with the untold than with the other crowd. Somewhere, someway, in God's time and wisdom, accounts will be settled. It's a frightening thought, but there's at least a chance that those beyond forgiveness – outside and untold – will put us beyond forgiveness. *Inasmuch as you did it not unto one of the least, you did it not unto Me.*

I Stand By The Door

BIRTHING BABY CHRISTIANS

The New Birth is in fact a <u>new</u> birth. A definite beginning of something incredibly different. This work of the Holy Spirit in the heart of a sinner is a result of repentance and turning to Christ for salvation. Sounds simple. Yet, church leaders are hard pressed to see an appreciable number of people evidence a spiritually transformed life. So many seekers at our public altars fail to translate into mature and productive Christian disciples. We must admit this has always been true to a degree, but it appears to have increased today. Unsaved people respond in public and personal evangelism yet fail to show interest in pursuing a Christian lifestyle. Even with a faithful pastor or layman making personal contact, so many do not become involved.

The reasons are many, I'm sure. While we all meet at the same level when we come to Christ, the environment prior to a seeking experience varies widely. The spiritual condition of the congregation is also a contributing factor. Only when the church is healthy and pregnant with the love of Christ, can she bring forth healthy children. Dead people do not reproduce naturally or spiritually. The church must also have Spirit-anointed people totally involved in assimilation programs for baby Christians. To assume new converts to Christ will find the food when we set the table spiritually is to underestimate, or ignore, discipleship.

Because of a lack of prior exposure, they may not recognize the food they need, and, in some churches, they can't get to the table. The saints have left no space. In other churches, the tables are empty.

I think there is another reason, and this goes much deeper. It will not be easily seen and very difficult to remedy. It may be that what we are offering, inadvertently, has diluted the experience of the New Birth. The unsaved must be confused when so many testify to a conversion experience while still living a life of sin. The all-inclusive philosophy, combined with religious tolerance at any cost, on the part of a large segment of the church, has done a number on the doctrine of the New Birth. Church attendance on Sunday morning with a Bible in our hand, is not necessarily an indication of a saved person. It doesn't take a rocket scientist to see that some models, even on the highest levels of national leadership, are horrid examples. And by the way, with the support of much of the contemporary church. The dilution of what an authentic salvation experience really is has clouded the issue and provided an array of substitutes.

<u>First</u>, <u>we</u> <u>are</u> <u>substituting</u> <u>renewal</u> <u>for</u> <u>conversion</u>. Across the church world, the call now is to renewal. Something or someone must be new before a renewal can occur. The intentions are good. It would be great to see a massive renewal movement across the world spiritually. But this does not really touch the unsaved where the disease of sin is lodged. Even an awakening would be more appropriate. The church does need a renewal or revival. No debate! A casual glance at the apathy and unconcern on the part of so many church members makes us aware of this problem. However, when an unsaved individual respond to a call for renewal, confusion is inevitable.

I Stand By The Door

He has had a moving experience, but realizes he is not functioning as a born-again Christian. Renewal is for the church – the New Birth is for the unsaved. Dry bones have been known to live again, but remember, they were once alive. God knows the countryside is littered with dry bones, but an unsaved person on the street, spiritually has never been. He can't be renewed. He must come alive by the New Birth.

<u>We are also substituting reformation for the New Birth</u>. The New Birth is self-enlisted, but not self-executed. It is supernatural. Reformation results from self-effort. The New Birth results from the work of the Holy Spirit in the human heart and mind. Reformation changes outward conduct. It's admirable! But, the New Birth changes character, our moral nature. Conversion to Christ is not a surface change, it's a radical transformation of our attitudes and interests. Reformation is a natural act, conversion to a follower of Jesus Christ is a supernatural work.

Sincere people bow at our altars, but a Divine transaction may not occur. When this happens, whatever the reason, they become even more difficult to reach. Is it possible that "reformers" are trying to lead them into the New Birth? By sheer human will, they themselves have made positive changes in their lives, but aren't familiar with the supernatural work of the Holy Spirit. While history has proved it is possible, it is very difficult to lead someone else where we've not been ourselves. Reformation has been used by our Lord in certain unique circumstances, but it isn't the New Birth.

<u>A regard and respect for the reality of Christ is a substitute for the New Birth</u>.

A mutual acknowledgement of Christ is not enough. Here is where many church members are satisfied to park.

We can believe. So does Satan. I'm sorry, but it is true. Simon, in Acts 8 believed, but he was not saved. We can believe He is powerful, yet not be a Christian. Some people are ready to die for Him but will not live for Him. We can give mental acknowledgement to Jesus' life, yet not experience salvation from sin. Saving faith is needed. This is a deliberate, conscious, personal act of believing not "things about Christ", but a conviction that He possesses the power <u>now</u> to forgive and re-create us in His moral image. A broad, general type of faith is a step toward God. But more specifically, we must possess saving faith.

We can believe He came, lived a sinless life, died on a cross, resurrected and went back to Heaven, from a mere historical basis. Thousands have and do. Saving faith goes farther. It is believing in our heart that for our sins He died, and for our justification He arose from the grave, and now He pardons and forgives. Regard for Christ may make us decent, but the New Birth delivers us from sin. Regard for Christ may make one different, but the New Birth makes us definite about our relationship with God.

<u>Finally, a resemblance to Christ can be a substitute for the New Birth</u>. Some people are just great to be around. Their personality is pleasing. They're not rude and even display an attitude of charity for the under privileged. It is not unusual to see them volunteer for the menial tasks around the church. They are honest and peace loving by nature. They are like the rich, young, ruler that came to Christ and said, "I've kept these commandments from my youth."

I Stand By The Door

But, he, like many today, walk away from a commitment to Christ. People can commit to a local church, yet not to Jesus Christ.

We must have more than a resemblance to Christ, we must be adopted into His family. *As many as received Him, to them He gave the power to become the sons of God, even to them that believe on His name. (John 1:12) You have not received the spirit of adoption again to fear; but you have received the spirit of adoption, whereby we cry Abba Father. (Romans 8:15)* Our parentage changes spiritually. We're no longer a child of Satan, but a child of God. We not only resemble Christ; we belong to the family through the experience of the New Birth.

I know it is not "correct" to be dogmatic today. To try to judge others has not been, nor is it now, the responsibility of we humans. So, what do we do about the disinterest and lack of commitment so prevalent in the church? We have some options. We could ignore it and keep the noise level acceptable. We could appoint a committee to research it, compile statistics, and give a report to someone important. Even publish it. At least in our own minds we could try to rationalize it away. We could get great comfort in labeling it "a sign of the times." We could compare ourselves with other churches that face the same problem. Or, we could take an honest, objective look at what we let pass for the experience of the New Birth.

I know I will incur the wrath of some for even thinking this, but maybe the church is at least part of the problem. In our effort to add to our membership rolls, we may have enclosed some "premature converts", or some "hot-house plants" that are not ready for the elements they will face.

Some of this may also be motivated by a desire to reach certain people of means and/or status. Once we've done this, we really don't know what to do with them.

One of two things normally occur. One, the New Birth bar is lowered to accommodate them. In education this is called the "dumbing-down of people", by some. The results have not been altogether good. Or, we could raise the bar for the New Birth. Maybe to where it, in reality, has always been. To offer a Christianity void of discipline and regime is fantasy at best and a cruel hoax at worst. True Christianity is a paradox. It's the toughest life to live, but no other way is as fulfilling. Christianity is the most challenging lifestyle but offers the greatest joy obtainable. It incurs the greatest storms yet settles the heart and provides a perfect inner peace.

Maybe if coming to Christ _really_ meant something, our seekers would rise to the challenge. Maybe if becoming a Christian _really_ meant an instantaneous life-changing experience, it would attract the masses. Perhaps, if no haziness existed in our presentation of a salvation experience there would be less hollowness in the hearts of our seekers. Could the lack of transformed, committed church members be attributed to "an uncertain sound" about conversion?

If we are somehow hoping the uncommitted will grow into a thriving, faithful, Christian disciple, without a New Birth, we ought to forget it. One can no more grow into a Christian than a pea can grow into a potato. We are either alive or dead spiritually. Not half-alive and half-dead! The authentic, scriptural, experience of the New Birth produces committed Christians in any age. Anything less may temporarily feed egos but will drive pastors up the wall.

In the process, our pews will be lined with people who do not have a clear witness of the Spirit that they are a child of God. Nor do they have a clue as to what they are supposed to be and how they are supposed to live. Based on much of what they see, it really may not matter.

The New Birth is a <u>New</u> Birth. The church should not involve itself in altering Christianity to suit people. People are to be altered to fit Christianity by a supernatural change by the Holy Spirit.

I Stand By The Door

ELIJAH: WORSHIP AND MANTLES

It was quite a scene! Elijah, the old prophet, was about to see His God move in a spectacular way once again. He had prayed for rain to cease years before, and a serious drought spread across the land. He prayed for God to send fire down on Mt. Carmel and it descended. After his long-awaited confrontation with King Ahab he announced a rain. The skies opened and water drenched the country. These, along with many other miracles, proved Elijah was familiar with the supernatural.

Now at the Jordan River, Elisha, his spiritual son, stood beside him. Elisha was about to watch something he would never forget. The sons of the prophets were nearby. Elijah called up his mantle, struck the Jordan and it divided. He and Elisha walked across. Elisha was impressed. Elijah looked at him and asked, "What may I do for you?" The young prophet must have thought, man, there may be some more Jordan's, I'm going for it. He said, "Let a double portion of your spirit be upon me." Elijah replied, "You ask a hard thing, and only God can grant such a request, but I'm leaving, and if you see me go it shall be done."

Suddenly a chariot and horses of fire separated them. Elijah was caught away by a whirlwind as Elisha watched. He was gone! Elisha picked up the mantle Elijah dropped, struck the waters of the Jordan and asked, "Where is the Lord God of Elijah?" The Jordan River divided again, and Elisha walked across.

Elisha was perceptive. He realized the power was not in Elijah's mantle, but in Elijah's God. The old mantle, probably a sleeveless garment, has gone the way of all the earth. It was what Elisha used at that moment. He, unlike so many others, did not make a shrine out of it. The mantle in the hands of Elisha was then only a symbol of a prophet's office. He knew this alone was not enough. He needed God Himself.

Across the years of church history, God's people have tended to "get caught up with mantles." We have difficulty understanding it is always God's presence, power, and our obedience that moves mountains and divides rivers, not mantles. His presence ensures life, mantles eventually die of old age. Some sooner than others. It is sad how we insist on propping up dead things. God's presence and power promotes church growth, mantles become heavy and divisive. It is a mature Christian that can separate the two.

The church is always in transition. The message can never change if the church is to survive. Lesser things come and go. The church is now in a struggle for and against change. It involves many areas, but much of the tension centers in worship style. It is ironic. True worship of God is our love for Him personally expressed in thought, word, and often music and song. It is now become a battleground. Of course, everyone is right, and we use nothing less than the Bible to prove it. It is a no-win situation, because in this setting God is not overly impressed with any particular camp. It should be a no-brainer. The mantle has become the issue and God does not care. That is a serious blow to most of us. However, it's impossible to truly worship a Creator God and at the same time feel superior to, or be critical of, another with a different worship style.

It is also ironic that we are now being schooled in how to worship. Some enjoy contemporary choruses and dislike old hymns. Others prefer the old hymns and feel uncomfortable with contemporary choruses. Some like the traditional piano and organ, and others like the keyboard, guitars, and drums. I suspect God could sanctify all of the above. The old hymns have weathered the tests of time and teach Bible doctrine. The contemporary choruses have words and music that encourage praise and worship. Mantles! And, mantles should never be allowed to divide God's family.

Hymnals have also become a source of contention. When you are not doing much, you must do or say something that will "make a statement" or find something to debate. It's happened. Some like hymnals, others prefer to sing with words on a public screen. Again, God doesn't care. I do believe if we are to sing from the screen, notes and words should be made available, lest we descend deeper into musical illiteracy. I must admit, if the print is large and clear enough it sure is easier to read from a screen at my age. Yet, I feel so secure with a hymnal in my hand. Oh! It is ridiculous! Everything we humans devise soon becomes another mantle.

We've heard it said, "If you want to complicate anything, put it in the hands of the government." While we all hope not, history has proved there is some truth in it. Maybe this could also be said about the church. I believe the church is the greatest institution in the world, but when she makes a concerted effort to explore or develop something, we tend to complicate it. We have worship leaders, worship pastors, worship teams, worship retreats and seminars, and only God knows what else. That's fine.

The intentions have been sincere, and in some cases helpful. But I have news! The intimacy between God and His children, in a moment of worship, is most sacred and personal. It transcends techniques. Any prodding for one certain worship style has to do with the human. It's shallow, and in this process, we are only enshrining another mantle, whether it be traditional or contemporary. Certainly, God trusts us to handle it. With our best minds and the Holy Spirit leading and teaching us, we will survive.

How quickly forms, methods, and rituals become mantles. It occurs when what _we_ do, however sincere, becomes greater than God. It occurs when what _we have_ designed or adopted becomes the issue and is permitted to become divisive. We have just enshrined mantles.

Churches, historically, seldom divide over doctrine or matters that will affect eternity. They often divide when methods and programs are deemed immortal. Sorry. There is only One Immortal and He is not about to leave His throne. He left a lot of this little stuff in our hands. We should not complicate it. As sacred and personal as worship is, we shouldn't fuss over how it should be done. Within certain doctrinal perimeters, to each his own. Frankly, I'm in a "straight betwixt two." I honestly like a little of traditional and the contemporary. Not a lot – but a little. I prefer not to be told how; I already know. It is a personal thing. Don't crowd me. I'll not be a problem to you.

Elijah's mantle was just an old garment. Old or often-used newer garments develop an unpleasant odor. It's not necessarily the age that causes the problem. They all need periodic inspection and probably cleansing. Do you detect an odor? If you do, you're probably not alone.

I Stand By The Door

All of us dislike mantles that get in our way when we want to worship God. He deserves our worship and I doubt if He considers any one-style superior. It is the attitude of the heart and mind. When that is right, He accepts our worship, whatever the mantle. When the attitude is wrong, the rest is only religious exercise.

If we could have "an instant replay" and project the prophet into our world today it would be interesting. One could imagine the sons of the prophets waxing eloquent about the mantle. I hear one say, "I have to believe the mantle would work better in daylight." Another steps up and says, "I've just come from a seminar and you're wrong, waters divide when soft music is playing in semi-darkness." I hear another say, "I'm fascinated with the mantle where in the greatest libraries of the world could one find the finest book on "The Origins of Mantles." One walks out of the crowd in a chapel service and disputes the others. I hear him say, "I've just had a revelation. It's not the mantle at all, it's the Jordan River. The waters were just right, evenly dividing each way. We must build three tabernacles here at the water's edge, make an intensive effort, and shift our emphasis to rivers." The whole assembly drops to their knees in earnest prayer for their fallen brother. He finally agrees. It's not the river, it's the mantle. There is nothing to do but perpetuate Elijah's mantle. Factories must be built to make Elijah mantles. We'll insist that they be in every church. Growth will come. We will commission great leaders to go out to conduct seminars and demonstrate Elijah mantles to the people. We will make a great profit for the Kingdom so we can send out more people to promote Elijah's mantles. Everyone should have the privilege to hear about Elijah's mantles at least once.

I Stand By The Door

Sad, isn't it? When it is so simple. *Give to the Lord the glory due His name: bring an offering and come before Him: worship the Lord in the beauty of holiness. (I Chronicles 16:29)*

That doesn't sound complicated. Certainly not divisive. I can do that. So, can you.

WHERE IS THE LORD GOD OF ELIJAH?

Where is the Lord God of Elijah? These words of Elisha, the new man on the prophet's road in a long-ago time, ring with relevance today. Sincere pastors and laymen, in a struggle for church growth, are asking the same question. Good News! The God of Elijah can always be the God of Elisha! *This God is our God, forever and ever, and He will be our Guide, even unto death. Psalm 48:14*

I have given much of my life to evangelism. But I suspect much of what is being said and written about the subject could lead one to believe ours is nearly a hopeless situation. While God is not considered dead, as earlier supposed, He is unwittingly portrayed as distant and uninvolved. The gulf between God and lost humanity is seen as deeper and wider than ever before. Could be.

Or, in observation, we could conjure up the picture of the Father so frustrated, He considers calling for a committee of angels to give advice. The Holy Spirit is on the sidelines wringing His hands, and Jesus has just gone away. We are led to believe only cleverly designed plans of an elite few, who totally understand the lost, can tear away the fabric that houses man's intellect and spirit. The road man must travel to reach God is such *that a wayfaring man, a disconnected being, cannot enter therein.* Nonsense!

These are indeed evil days. Our own nation is in a moral free-fall. Wall Street out-influences Straight Street in our trade of morality for money.

I Stand By The Door

While we wallow in pride over human achievements, fear and anxiety eats away at our inner structure. Our word and sacred covenants are only things to discard when inconvenient. Disregard for human life has produced the death of millions of unborn children. Others born are a nuisance in countless American homes. Alcoholism and drug addiction have turned our communities and schools into war zones.

Truth is not necessarily truth. Right can be wrong, and wrong can be right. The shameless debacle on the national scene reveals who and what we really are. And, in a weird scramble for acceptance by those who should not matter, much of the church has positioned herself in a bland, non-confrontational mode. Tolerance is more important than truth.

The liberal crowd has more clout than God's crowd in government. Only practicing Christians can be openly ridiculed without arousing the wrath of our leaders and the media. Man is a long way from God. But, for the sake of Christ and lost people, let up. The point has been made. No contest. Enough!

Maybe we've never been here before in all human history. Possible. At the same time, we have never had a couple of generations so deeply analyzed and defined. We've all but memorized the Thirty-Plus characteristics of the Boomers. What Generation X likes, and dislikes has been ably and often articulated. We are now aware of their battles and baggage. Thanks for the extensive research. I personally owe a debt for the work done. Our eyes have been opened to new and exciting possibilities for evangelism.

But, the human race didn't wait with bated breath for you to come. Nor did they wait until now to produce people with the same characteristics.

I Stand By The Door

Most every family has some that turned out this way. In any event, if a child is told he or she is either good or bad often enough, over a long enough period of time, chances are it will come true. The same could probably be said about a generation. Maybe it has. Maybe it is worth a thought.

Change and hardship did not have its genesis in the last few years. This is not the first generation to enter life on an uphill road. Another generation keeps hanging around. They suffered the hurts of two World Wars, not to mention those of recent years. Mothers, for the first time, walked out of the house and entered the workplace. The economy collapsed and local banks closed in a day. Private property, held in trust for generations, was lost. Families were uprooted and migrated from rural America to the cities. People were on the streets begging for food and a place to stay while searching for employment. Scars remain. Most generations have felt the sting of life's realities. So, accept them today and move on. Get a life. Someone is following you. They will probably blame you for the way they feel.

Amid all of this, we should not fear what is new. It seems the Church is the most difficult institution to change. The reason something has never been done may be the reason it should be done. I'm not speaking for those who want change for change sake. They were probably unruly children too. Their mindset has limited their potential. Life to them has been a revolving door and they cannot remember where they started or their destination.

Yet, if corporations fail to innovate, they are destined for either bankruptcy or being swallowed by a merciful competitor. If the Church is to succeed in reaching the lost, it will mean innovation.

I Stand By The Door

A word to the wise, *If it isn't broke, don't fix it*, even to have the smile of someone with a packed portfolio.

Confusion has surfaced over the marketing of new things in the Church. It is evidenced in a sense of helplessness and discouragement. Caught between a hunger to evangelize, and guilt for not producing a harvest, pastors and laymen feel they have failed. For so long and often they have been told their approach is wrong, sometimes from unqualified messengers. Dropping what they have been somewhat successful doing, they comply. For whatever reason it not only failed to produce growth, they've lost ground. The loud testimonials about those who have succeeded have only intensified their frustration.

Much of what is being communicated is negative. What does not produce. It supplies information for humorous stories and sells well. Yet, little that has substance is offered to those who need it most. Pastors and laymen close out a week's ministry with a heavy sense of defeat.

If evangelism and church growth is too complicated for the average person – it is too complicated. When evangelism becomes a science, little evangelism occurs. When 70% to 80% of church growth comes from membership transfer, and it does, it should raise concern. We all know what is not producing. What will? And, it must have substance and handles for churches without a paid staff, or people give up. Churches die. Communities are unreached – untouched. The prospect for present and future Christian workers will indeed be dim.

Our opportunities are incredible. Despite all that is wrong, people hunger for God. Millions will fall asleep tonight with uneasiness and fear.

I Stand By The Door

They are frustrated and insecure. Many are hostile and bitter. Tomorrows bring dread. Days are pressure packed. Employers and employees are tough, calculating and cold. Adults and children long for some identity and acceptance. Success and possessions are a bittersweet reward for years of service. From CEO's to the homeless, life for some is a cruel joke – a story with an inevitable bad ending.

Into this swirling cauldron of humanity, the Church must go. It is possible that our society finally is a reprint of the past. Maybe there is hope. Maybe a fire can ignite once again in the heart of a discouraged pastor or layman. Maybe there is a simple plan somewhere to reach the lost.

I re-read about a time that was tough for the Church. Human slavery was rampant. Only certain people were considered worth anything, and few were ever expected to have contact with God. Children were sacrificed to pagan gods. Other children, with imperfections, were treated like refuse. Divorce was readily permitted if a more attractive subject appeared. Womanhood, by our standards, was worse than second class. The blind and crippled begged on roads and streets.

Wicked and abusive rulers reigned. Injustice was expected. Violence and death hit every home. Diseases had no cures. Perversion of all sorts infected society. Murder, rape, and incest were common. Children of fathers with multiple wives were born into an atmosphere that engendered low self-esteem, jealousy and hatred. Poverty was the lot of the majority. And the Church was proud and disconnected.

But, Jesus came! With a simple, but demanding message. For everyone.

I Stand By The Door

He lived among them and taught a few. He tried to train them, but they didn't understand. He was rejected by the Church. They finally had Him killed. But He arose and told His disciples not to leave Jerusalem until they were empowered by the Spirit. They waited and on the Day of Pentecost, they received the promise. They left the place where they were gathered and began evangelizing. From Jerusalem to Samaria – on and on to the end of the earth. The government was disgusted with them and the religious leaders wanted them destroyed. Some were.

This revolutionary message leaped language, social, economic, political, and religious barriers. Lives were radically changed. Things were still tough. Life was uncertain. Wickedness remained. Cruel and crooked leaders still reigned. But Jesus changed people through people – one on one. They reproduced. It was a simple plan. Centuries of converts validate its value. People filled with Christ's love, with an all-consuming desire to win souls, are still around today. Lives are being changed!

Where is the Lord God of Elijah as we close out Century 20? He is here with us. Pastor – layman – you can do it! It may have to be done your way. Perhaps you do not understand the culture and personality of those you long to win. Always search for better tools. The distance man must travel to get to God may be farther than it's ever been. So what? God knows. But, don't buy into anything that would tend to limit the power of the Holy Spirit in evangelism.

May you become so in love with Jesus that you begin to weep Calvary-like tears over the lost. Cultivate a burning heart.

I Stand By The Door

Give me a choice between a man with all the tools without a burning heart, and one struggling with his tools with a burning heart. I'll always join the latter. The ideal is to possess both. Few do.

A burning heart will cause us to love those Jesus loves. When we do, we determine to reach them. We'll find a way. New babies will be born into the Kingdom. Our churches will be exciting and grow. New recruits will volunteer to enter the harvest. What could not be done is being done. God is pleased and angels rejoice. Our life is filled with purpose and satisfaction. And one day in that other land, we'll stand at attention and watch the new arrival in that magnificent procession of the redeemed. We'll pause to reflect. I helped win him. I witnessed to her. I prayed. We will know for certain - it was worth it all.

Where is the Lord God of Elijah? He's waiting for someone – anyone, who will settle for nothing but a perfect love for God and people, and – just do it! By the way, Elisha picked up Elijah's mantle, smote the waters, and walked across the river. You can too.

I Stand By The Door

WE GET WHAT WE REALLY WANT

Why is my church so small? So often, I'm faced with this question. Another, more positive question I hear is, "How can my church grow?" Most pastors and laymen want to be a part of a thriving, expanding body of believers. They sincerely want to impact their community. They also want their family and friends to be a part of their church. Looking in from the outside a more relevant question is, "Do we want to grow enough to pay whatever price it will take?"

Most of us are followers, and that ironically, can be a part of the problem in a non-growing church. Most every church is the product of past leaders. It has been shaped and influenced by people from previous generations. Good or bad. Most church boards are made up of members who were highly influenced by certain pastors and lay leaders. Every member reflects leadership and personalities that will determine his philosophy of the church. So, if a church remains small, some characteristics that have reproduced will have to be faced before it can move into a growth mode. It will be a painful process of "disowning and owning." An honest view of reality will no doubt reveal some concepts that must undergo change. It will take our best to do it.

The attitude of a local church helps govern its size. Herein lies a serious challenge, because most churches believe their attitudes are right.

What we say and what we are may differ. It's in the eye of the beholder. A critical attitude is highly contagious. Criticism can start with one person, spread through a group, and ultimately cripple the efforts of a congregation. A critical spirit gives birth to non-cooperation, and this becomes defeatism. The prayers, witnessing, public services, and the general tone of the church will turn negative. What starts as a small spark, explodes into a fire that envelopes the body of believers. A critical attitude not only endangers growth, it paralyzes the will to grow. The reason? The church becomes introverted. Thoughts center on itself. Most of the energy and dollars are spent in a self-absorbed mentality. When a church is disgruntled and defending philosophies that have kept it small, outreach is not a high priority. Add to this the inevitable power struggle in such situations, it's little wonder no growth occurs.

A positive attitude on the other hand is also contagious. It lifts and breeds enthusiasm. Success is determined by our attitudes, and our attitudes determine our actions. Right attitudes tend to be positive toward others, so outreach becomes natural. It's true we can be positive about wrong things, but it's only an effort to compensate for a negative.

Authentic New Testament churches are blessed with people that are not driven by negatives. Their attitudes are wholesome. They're loving and considerate of others. These people take pride in their church. Instead of murmuring, they pray. Instead of criticizing, they affirm. Small wonder a church grows with such members. Attitudes govern the size of churches. Churches with positive and holy attitudes attract non-church people. They are their own greatest advertisement.
People may gather weekly in Jesus' name with negative attitudes, but they can't be a growing body of believers in the New Testament tradition. Wrong

attitudes endanger the health of a congregation, right attitudes engender hope and harmony. Churches become well known as to their personality. How about you and yours?

Our concept of authority governs the size of local churches. Much of what is called "a smorgasbord mentality" about where we go to church has to do with authority. A church made up of people that refuse to participate in ministry is a church with little respect for authority. That body of believers cannot reach their full spiritual potential. The Bible clearly teaches obedience and respect for those in charge. It also teaches the value of unity. A house divided cannot stand, and a church without respect for authority is a house divided.

I cannot speak for others, but there is an alarming trend among church leaders. And, it didn't start last week. It would be interesting to observe a roll call for ministers. The gap between those credentialed and those subscribing to denominational responsibilities would not paint an encouraging scene. To fail as ministers to come under authority reproduces the same in laymen. We may well have a double standard. Preachers expect compliance and respect in local churches yet fail to come under denominational authority. Elected laymen can hardly be expected to participate. And many don't.

Church leader, you are doing an amazing job of teaching on how you do, or do not, come under authority. You are being followed. Don't be surprised when they walk in your footsteps on the local level.

Churches remain small, or at least plateau, over a lack of respect for authority. By the way, there isn't such a commodity as an authentic, independent church. No

New Testament church is sovereign. We must all come under the authority and leadership of Jesus Christ. A church, in or out of a denomination that does not subscribe to this has no part in the Christian tradition. A New Testament church is one that is team oriented. Someone with a healthy respect for authority is the leader. That church can experience sustained growth.

Why is respect for authority pertinent to a growing church? Finally, it has to do with evangelism. Jesus said, *To go into all the world and preach the gospel to every creature. (Mark 16:15)* The response of much of the church is "no." When we do not respect human leaders, we probably will not respect God. Tough words! But, when we fail to come under authority as leaders, we reproduce. The bottom line is, we've raised people that do not even remotely consider spiritual reproduction. The answer is "no." Oh, some get sentimental and give offerings to foreign mission fields, and we should, but will not evangelize people on their street. Consequently, churches struggle to hold on to the people they now have. Our response to authority affects the size of churches.

<u>The activities of a local church govern its size</u>. Few would question that the purpose of the church is to reach lost people for Christ. We are to win, and disciple converts. We know we should nurture and lead them into the experience of entire sanctification. And, we are to "make converters out of our converts." So, why aren't many churches growing? Evidently, what we are doing doesn't synchronize with the mission statement. An active church is not always a growing church.

A pastor spoke to me recently with concern about the lack of growth in his church over a long period of time.

I Stand By The Door

We talked and I encouraged him to continue praying about it, compile some information, and humbly present his findings to the church board in their next meeting. He agreed. Sometime later we were together. I asked him about it. He said, "our time was taken up with other things and it was too late."

Some good activities are a hindrance to church growth. Too many meetings "close with no time left for the main 'point'." Board meeting minutes tell the story of what we really believe and do. Our passion for involvement in secondary matters leaves little time for evangelism. Every scheduled activity should be under the umbrella of reaching people for Christ. Our music and singing. Children's Church should witness conversions. Sunday School classes ought to be considered mission fields, for some are. ECY services should put evangelism at the center. The "spark" in local churches often evolves from youth. Senior citizens shouldn't lose the fire of evangelism. In fact, they should act the example. If retirement destroys the love for souls, it is a bad thing.

Everything in our public services should be geared to reaching people. This will not just happen. No longer can we just schedule without planning for something to happen. This does not bypass the leadership of the Spirit. On the contrary, one of the reasons churches do not grow is due to the dearth of expectancy. The Holy Spirit expects us to carefully and prayerfully plan. We usually get what we go after. If we do not expect conversions and other miracles, they probably won't happen.

<u>Christ's accessibility governs the size of churches</u>. How far do people have to travel to get to Christ in our churches?

I Stand By The Door

The message may be out of reach for the average person on the street. Every church believes their church is friendly when it could be described as a "closed circuit." We are friendly, I would hope with one another. Maybe too friendly for an outsider-visitor. People cemented to the corner of the pews say to them "off limits." Ushers pointing them to a "much despised and empty front pew", has caused many not to ever return. I've talked to too many people who visited a public service in camps and local churches for the first time and never returned because of unfriendliness. Some of them are now prominent leaders in other denominations. Others "slipped through the cracks." To them, at least in their minds, Christ is out of reach.

The truth is, "Christ is chained!" To public pulpits. To programs that are at best exclusive. To church members that feel little personal responsibility to bring Christ down within reach of unsaved people. The message of Christ is to be made accessible. Only that church that builds this truth into their mentality and philosophy can expect to impact people positively. So much of what we do comes through as tired and monotonous to the lost. If we will "unchain Jesus", He will bring excitement. Nothing helps a church like watching Him transform new converts.

We put Christ out of reach when we confine our message to a "social-feel good" gospel. Christianity deals with sin in the human heart. Jesus came to *"preach deliverance to the captives, not to make them feel better in their prison."* Much of what is going on in churches has to do with surface issues. It will attract a crowd temporarily. But, when Monday morning comes, they are still searching. And, when another bigger and better program comes across town, these people will leave. Surface ministries deal with surface needs.

I Stand By The Door

Until people find healing for where they hurt, the hunger goes on. The mystery is, churches that have been offering this over the long haul are being emptied, and they have become our models. It's maddening!

Christ also becomes inaccessible when we fail to exemplify Him in our lives. The greatest single hindrance to growing churches is a nonchalant, spiritually impoverished, professing Christian. An apathetic, defeated minister or layman puts Christ out of reach of people. Sometimes it's not that the unsaved won't come to church, we drive them away. Our refusal to objectively suspect our methods, and change if necessary, to reach them, make Jesus inaccessible. When programs are designed only for the saved, He is out of reach. When tradition supersedes or becomes the message, our Lord is chained. Release Him. Bring Him down, within reach of the lost!

Churches fail to grow because of their inaccessibility. In the real estate market, it's location, location, location. But our problem has little to do with location, in most cases. It has to do with good people that have become greedy with Jesus Christ. An old truth is, "if we fail to share Him, we lose Him." That may be a whole new idea for contemporary holiness people that have bought into a "version of unconditional eternal security" upon being entirely sanctified. Think about it.

Some of the fastest growing churches in America are not in suburbia with sprawling campuses.
They are bottled up in inner cities. People walk through trash and garbage on the street, observe heinous crimes, and wind their way through unbelievable traffic to find them. But they're exploding numerically and impacting countless lives and homes.

I Stand By The Door

Why? Because they are making Christ accessible to people. Christ, properly presented, is always attractive. He fixes what is wrong with spiritually diseased humanity.

Churches grow when the leadership and members want it enough to change. If a non-growing church isn't willing to change, the past will paint a graphic picture of its future – if it survives at all. I'm not advocating a contemporary worship style over the traditional. Both tell some scary stories, and both have successes. We get what we go after, and the wrapping should not become the issue. Christ is bigger than our Sunday ceremonials, however, correct. And He is bigger than anything we cloak Him in. Release Him! Turn Him loose!

I almost forgot. He did say, *I will build my church.* *(Matthew 16:18)* Let's quit fussing, get rid of the baggage we've gathered, and let Him – through us. Without Him we don't have much going for us.

A COMMON PRAYER FOR THE UNCOMMON

Dear God, you can't be serious! In my devotions this morning, I have read some startling words. I don't wish to come across irreverently, but was Peter translating you correctly? *But, be ye holy now in everything you do, just as the Lord is holy.* Who invited you to be His child? He then quotes you directly, *Ye must be holy, for I am holy. I Peter (1:15-16)* I was also reminded of something you said while you were here with us, *But you are to be perfect even as your Father in heaven is perfect. (Matthew 5:48)* Compared to You Lord, we don't have a chance. Do we? I hear it isn't even expected of us now. Things being as they are. Maybe back in Peter's time the situation was different. You could have preserved them in a capsule-like environment, insulated from the evil world. And, perhaps Satan is intensifying his efforts today against us. So, the doctrine of perfection and holiness are obsolete. Unattainable. Right?

If so, you may want to send an addendum to your Word in some dramatic way. This will make it applicable to our generation. Maybe in bold print across the sky, understandable in every language. Then we would know you have relaxed your earlier standards. We do have something very helpful in communication today. It is the computer. Your writers never heard of it.

You may wish to check it out, get on what we call the Internet and get a website. Or, we also have what we call E-mail. With such tools, you could reach a lot of people quickly.

They in turn could inform the rest of the world. But you'll know how to handle it. Maybe just a revision or even a disclaimer as to this matter of being perfect and holy.

But God, what if Peter's words are up to date? In effect yet today? Doesn't change with the times? What if from the dawn of creation, it has been and is Your will for us to be made holy? If it is correct, then we are to walk before you, and our fellowmen, with a pure heart. Mankind was originally created holy, but with a choice about it. He fell from that lovely state of grace upon disobedience to Your commands. God, I know you didn't will that the first parents in Eden sin against you. They chose. But, in your perfect wisdom you knew it would occur. You made a wonderful plan to reconcile them and us. And, according to Peter, and many other writers, you also made provision for redeemed souls to be restored to a holy position again. God, if what was in effect still is, we need to know.

And Lord, there is something else we need to discuss. We now have psychology. It has compounded the problem of sin in the human heart. One side reads all behavior as nothing more than a mechanical response to environmental stimuli. Others vehemently disagree and read all our wrongs as the result of moral failure. So, one side tells us the bad things we do are not our fault. Some kind of collision occurred in our past and that is the problem. Why we do what we do. Both sides are adamant, but I think somewhat confused. God, no one seems to know in this camp when, or if, the "normal reactions" ever interact with sin. Lord, we're in a lot of trouble here. Maybe an addendum is needed. You told us not to add or take away from your Word. So, if you don't act on this, any change will not be authentic.

I Stand By The Door

Seems like we're taking it upon ourselves to initiate change, so help us. Please!

And, God, I must be honest. I can read what Peter and others wrote and understand it. *Just be holy – perfect.* But we only tend to complicate it. So many terms and words. We are mired in terminology. I must wonder if they really understand it. Or, believe it's possible. They can't say it clearly. To be candid, I often must go back to your book to find out where they are. They mean well. But most of what they write and say never reaches common people on the street like me. It's all stuff. For debate, and so defensive most of the time. Why do they do this? Help me, if you can. They have succeeded in doing what Satan cannot do. They have turned what sounds to me like the most beautiful and helpful experience into something that comes across boring and intellectual. Hard to understand, and maybe, according to many, impossible. They don't agree. Some believe this something that's wrong with me is a substance to be moved somewhere else or pushed out of sight. It happens in a crisis, or a life-long process. Could it be both, God?

This morning I see you as Creator. You understand our plight. How far Adam fell, and the results of such tragedy. We have inherited his sinful nature. This I know. I sense a tendency not to do what is good and right and see some things about myself that I detest. The self-life in me is corrupt. I'm saved, but I see something in me that strives against you. One man wrote about this. "Prone to wonder, Lord I feel it, prone to leave the God I love." (Charles Wesley) I read where the stream of human life was corrupted at the headwaters – the fountain where our first parents sinned. That evil, rebellious nature has spilled into the heart of us all. God, if it has been translated correctly, we don't have to remain as we are.

I Stand By The Door

You told us to be holy. In your prayer to the Father you said to Him, *Sanctify them or make them holy. (John 17:17)* So, we cannot make ourselves holy. God, you have to do it. You also desire all of us to be in unity down here. *That they all may be one; as Thou Father, art in Me, and I in Thee, that they may become one in Us. (John 17:21)*

Lord, that's tough. But for one or two I probably could. This evidently reaches into every compartment of life. *You said, Follow peace with <u>all</u> men, and holiness without which no man shall see the Lord. (Hebrews 12:14)* God, that's straight and clear! We can't do it ourselves, but we have a part. But, this matter of living in peace and a state of holiness is a tall order. What about our homes? My spouse doesn't seem to understand that I never speak until I know I'm right. Children don't seem to understand me. Nor I them. Some are wired to some "outernet." Totally oblivious to the real world. In response to a statement or question, they move their shoulders and mouth that means something. What, I'm not sure. Harmony in the home? Like between you and the Father? Help me God!

Now the church. Not everyone agrees with me. I do what I think is right. Form great opinions, obviously inspired. Run into every conceivable theology in one week. None are wrong – including me. Right? Even how to do church work is complicated. Here again, I've prayed through on how it should be done. Others disagree. Have unity and harmony like you and the Father? Lord, holy living is tough under these circumstances.
If you would just make other people agree with me, the road would be much easier to travel. Not going to happen.

I Stand By The Door

But, dear God, I somehow believe what Peter wrote was correct. It's a part of your plan. Whatever it takes, it is better than any alternatives I know about. If it's your desire that I be a holy person, I want to be. That's what I want more than anything else. If I cannot do it by myself, and I know I can't, I place myself in Your hands. I'm willing to do what I can. My heart cannot rest until I rest completely on You. Here and now not knowing what else I can do, I consciously let loose of selfish ambitions and self-centeredness that have been a part of me. But, most of all, my will, I turn over the control of myself – everything I have and am.

God, I don't want to get confused with a lot of theological jargon. That's been part of the problem. I want to be holy and have a pure heart. Until all of my attitudes and motives will be filtered through Your perfect will. I understand that I won't be faultless, but I deeply wish to be blameless in Your eyes. I may not always satisfy You, but God, I want to please You. God, please make my heart holy, like Yours. There's no way my capacity equals Yours, but may it be filled with purity of intent.

Lord, show me when I fail You and others. Keep me pure. I will to do this. Please, make me holy. When it comes to perfection, and this is not easy to understand, I do believe it has to do with the qualitive, not quantitive. "Pressing toward the mark" I know is a part of the long process. But, Lord, here today I've reached a place, a milestone, when I surrender my all to You. And, I do! Now!

Please God, give me the words to help others to do the same – simple words that do not confuse, complicate, or frustrate. Thank You, Lord, for helping me today.

I Stand By The Door

HOPELESSNESS!

A thin, ragged, dirty-faced boy sits in the shadow of a mud hut. The sun is scorching hot and the only comfort this little boy knows as he sits there is the light breeze and the shade. He's hungry and he's not alone. A pitiful cry comes from inside the hut. A step closer lets us see the dirt floor and more children. A haggard-looking mother tries desperately to calm the one who cries. Smoke curls up from the fire in one end where the mother is doing her best to prepare what little she has for a meal. She has no help now because her husband met with a tragic accident leaving her a widow with six small undernourished children.

There's something about this whole scene that bothers me. I stand there wondering what it is I see written on the face of this mother and the crying child, the others inside and yes, this little ragged, dirty-faced boy sitting there just staring into space. He doesn't seem to know anyone else is around. His whole world is within just a few feet of him. What is that on their faces? It isn't hate or bitterness. I've never seen this look before. I must know . . . and now! I start to walk away.

Just then the boy looked up . . . and oh, those eyes! I can never forget them. He doesn't say a word, but oh, the message those eyes conveyed! I know what it is I see on their faces.

It's <u>hopelessness</u>! Reminds me of a whimpering pup that's been whipped by its master. You know . . . that "hurt look." I suddenly realize there are human beings in this world who really "hurt" with no one to love them. Some have never had a good meal or slept on a clean bed. This hurting is utter "hopelessness." No plans because they have no hope. They never expect to live better, just suffering the awful, knowing pains of hopelessness.

That look isn't there just because of material wants. They're hungry in a far deeper way. They've never one time heard the name of Jesus or listened to a song of hope. There's something that craves satisfaction. It's that part of us, and yes, even this family in this hard, ruthless, civilization, that reaches toward and cries for God. This mother and her children are starving for fellowship with their Creator, but the tragedy is, they've never heard of Him. No one has told them that this God-like part of us can be satisfied. They only know of the intense hunger. No missionary has ever been here.

I fell upon my knees there in the dust of the road. Hot tears race down my cheeks because this little boy is not ragged and dirty to me now. I see a precious child with eyes that tell me he's hungry. I see a gem – a priceless gem, worth more than a thousand worlds. I see a soul who until now was hopeless. But oh, I can help him! I call him over to me and pull him close and say, "Son, Jesus loves you and I love you too.

I Stand By The Door

Jesus became poor that He might make you rich. He died so you could really live. Jesus can help that 'hurt' on the inside."

I watch his little eyes brighten . . . the old faraway look leaves. He jerks away leaving me there on my knees in the dust. I listen as he calls his mother and relates to her what I had just told him. Tears come to her eyes as he talks, and a new look appears on her face. God changed that little mud hut into a grand palace that day and healed a family of hopelessness, Jesus came there to live.

Then, I awoke and looked around. It was my home. Had this been only a dream? Yes, it was. For a moment I had been a missionary somewhere and had helped Jesus to reach that family. Down beside my bed I fell and began to pray. Not as I had prayed before, but really praying. "God, help me to never miss a chance to help someone to hear about Jesus. Don't ever let me forget that look of hopelessness in the eyes of that little boy. If you can't send me there . . . let me help here that someone <u>can</u> go and give hope to the hopeless."

Hopelessness is a terrible thing. Only God can relieve it and God can only work as we work.

I Stand By The Door